A Dictionary of
**Basic
Japanese
Sentence
Patterns**

A Dictionary of
Basic
Japanese
Sentence
Patterns

Naoko Chino

KODANSHA INTERNATIONAL
New York • Tokyo • London

Distributed in the United States by Kodansha America, Inc., and in the
United Kingdom and continental Europe by Kodansha Europe Ltd.

Published by Kodansha International Ltd., 17-14 Otowa 1-chome,
Bunkyo-ku, Tokyo 112-8652, and Kodansha America, Inc.

ISBN 4-7700-2608-0

First edition, 2000
10 09 08 07 06 05 04   15 14 13 12 11 10 9 8 7 6

www.thejapanpage.com

CONTENTS

N1 and N2 are N3.

2. N1 と N2 は Adj です。
N1 to N2 wa Adj desu.
N1 and N2 are Adj.

CHAPTER **3** Basic Patterns 6-14

CHAPTER **2** **Basic Patterns 19-22** 147

N does not V. / N will not V.

CHAPTER **3** Basic Patterns 23-27   168

CHAPTER **6**   Basic Patterns 42-46   239

N1 は / が N2 を / に V
   (causative) ます。
N1 wa / ga N2 o / ni
   V(causative)-masu.
N1 makes N2 do V.

N1 は / が N2 を / に N3 を V
   (causative) ます。
N1 wa / ga N2 o / ni N3 o
   V(causative)-masu.
N1 makes N2 do V N3.

V(causative-passive)-masu
N1 は N2 に V (causative-pas-
   sive) ます。
N1 wa N2 ni V(causative-pas-
   sive)-masu.
N1 is made to do V by N2.

N1 は N2 に N3 を V (causative-
   passive) ます。
N1 wa N2 ni N3 o V(causative-
   passive)-masu.
N1 is made to do V N3 by N2.

Appendices   273

PREFACE

The purpose of this dictionary is to help students gain a better grasp of the basic sentence patterns of the Japanese language, either by refreshing their knowledge of what has been learned in the past or by acquainting themselves with new patterns. The dictionary contains fifty basic patterns and explains and exemplifies them through example sentences. When there are variations on these basic patterns, they are also explained and exemplified. The book can be used purely for reference or it can be read profitably from beginning to end as a textbook. The latter method has the benefit of fixing the patterns in the student's mind by means of repetition.

There are three basic types of Japanese sentences that form the basis for the entire language; all the other sentence patterns and variations contained in this dictionary are based on one or another of these three. Once the student has become completely familiar with these patterns, the other patterns and variations based upon them should not be difficult to pick up. These three basic sentence patterns are as follows:

The Three Basic Sentence Patterns
    Noun Sentence
    Adjective Sentence
    Verb Sentence

In a noun sentence, it is the noun at the end of the sentence, followed by *desu* in polite usage, that provides information about the subject. In the following example, *book* tells you what *this* is; that is, *book* is acting as the predicate, providing information about the subject.

これは<u>本</u>です。
Kore wa <u>hon</u> desu.
This is a <u>book</u>.

In an adjective sentence, the part of the sentence providing information about the subject ("he") is an adjective (followed by *desu* in polite usage).

彼は<u>若い</u>です。
Kare wa <u>wakai</u> desu.
He is <u>young</u>.

In a *verb sentence*, the part of speech providing information about the subject ("she") is a verb.

彼女は<u>食べます</u>。
Kanojo wa <u>tabemasu</u>.
She <u>eats</u>. / She will <u>eat</u>.

Noun and adjective sentences are dealt with in Part 1; verb sentences in Part 2. All patterns are exemplified in polite and informal usage, sometimes in language that is characteristic of either male or female speech. Using the sentences above, polite and formal usage might be exemplified as follows:

Noun Sentence

Polite

これは本です。
Kore wa hon desu.

Informal

これは本 (だ)。
Kore wa hon (da).

In the case of informal adjective sentences, na-adjectives (see Basic Pattern 2) are optionally followed by *da* but i-adjectives, as in the following example, are not.

Adjective Sentence

Polite

彼は若いです。
Kare wa wakai desu.

Informal

彼は若い。
Kare wa wakai.

In a verb sentence, polite usage calls for the *masu* form of the verb, while informal usage calls for the plain form. (See the Verb Conjugation Chart at the back of the book for examples of both.)

Verb Sentence

Polite

彼女は食べます。
Kanojo wa tabemasu.

Informal

彼女は食べる。
Kanojo wa taberu.

Informal usage is usually not given in books like the present one. By providing it as a point of reference, even though commentary is limited owing to space considerations, we hope that students who come in contact with it in daily life or in their reading will find its inclusion here of some help.

Another feature of this dictionary is the use of a "formula" to provide information on the structure of the basic pattern under consideration. For example, the formula of the sentence 彼は日本人です (*Kare wa Nihon-jin desu*) would be appear as follows:

Formula

> <u>N1</u> wa <u>N2</u> desu.
> N1 = a noun acting as a subject
> N2 = a noun providing information about the subject

Students who have some familiarity with the basics of Japanese can refer to these formulas to reinforce their understanding or check areas they are unsure of. By inserting their own words in the underlined slots indicating parts of speech, students can expand their range of expression. For example, by placing *watashi* ("I") in the N1 slot and various other nouns concerning oneself in the N2 slot (e.g., name, nationality, occupation), students can easily create sentences that could serve as a self-introduction.

<u>私</u>は<u>田中</u>です。
Watashi wa Tanaka desu.
I'm Mr. Tanaka.

私は<u>アメリカ人</u>です。
Watashi wa Amerika-jin desu.
I'm an American.

私は<u>銀行員</u>です。
Watashi wa ginkō-in desu.
I'm a bank employee.

Students who are just starting out in their study of Japanese might try the following: find in this dictionary the basic sentence you are studying in your school textbook, read the explanation, and then substitute words for the underlined elements so that you create a sentence that expresses what you wish to say. By using even one basic pattern, you can create a variety of sentences.

The conjugation of verbs has not been discussed in this book because that topic would take up entirely too much space. However, I have covered verbs in the Power Japanese title *Japanese Verbs at a Glance*. Please refer to that book if you need help with conjugation. This dictionary does contain, however, charts at the end to be used as quick-reference guides to verb conjugation and adjective inflection. Students who need help with particles might refer to my *All about Particles*.

While the basic patterns in this book are not comprehensive in their coverage, they do represent many of the most common patterns. In fact, all of the patterns needed for passing levels 3 and 4 of the Japanese Language Proficiency Test are included. Moreover, many of the basic patterns have variations that also receive individual treatment in this dictionary. Among the patterns not included, such as past tense variations, some have been intentionally excluded because they can be easily surmised from the given patterns.

Finally, the student should check the section entitled "Abbreviations and Definitions" before proceeding to the main text.

* * *

It is my hope that this dictionary will be of help to students of Japanese. I would like to thank Shigeyoshi Suzuki and Michael Brase at Kodansha International for not only encouraging me to write the book but providing invaluable help in bringing it to final form.

Naoko Chino
Tokyo
2000

まえがき

　この辞典は日本語学習に役立つ基礎的な50の文型とそれらの変化型を構造と機能の上から簡潔に説明した文型集です。構文の理解を助け、より実用性を持たせるため、全ての文型に例文を付け、かつ各文型の例文を「です／ます」体を使ったていねいな表現 (Polite) と、友達や家族の間で使う会話体(Informal)の二通りとし、構文の骨格をより理解しやすいよう配慮しました。初級学習者にとって特に会話体は省略した表現や簡便な言い回しのため文章構造の認識が難しい上に、通常初級のテキストにはあまり会話体が登場することがないため一層馴染みにくいものとなっています。同一の文型をformalな表現と informalな表現で確認することができる本書は、辞書としてばかりでなく学習書としても大いに役立つことと思います。

　文型は大きく三つに分けています。「名詞型」、「形

容詞型」、「動詞型」がそれで、名詞型は「田中さんは学生です」のように文章が名詞で終わるもの。形容詞型は「田中さんは若いです」のように形容詞で、動詞型は「田中さんは歩きます」のように動詞で終わるものを指します。

各項目の文型紹介は、たとえば次のようにされます。

N1 wa N2 desu.
N1 is N2.
N1 = noun (subject)
N2 = noun (predicate)

ある程度初級段階の勉強をした学習者は文型のNのところの単語を入れ替えていろいろな文章を作成練習する事により表現が広がっていきます。
　例えば、上にあげた文型を用いて自分の名前、国籍、職業などをNに入れると、自己紹介が簡単にできます。

　私は田中です。　（名前）
　私は日本人です。（国籍）
　私は銀行員です。（職業）

従いまして、本辞典は、不確かだったところを確かめることができるばかりでなく、自分が学習したことをワークブック的な使い方で役立てることができます。

　日本語の形容詞と動詞は文型によって変化が起きます。変化の仕方については、この本の巻末に動詞と形容詞の活用表を載せてありますので、そちらを参照してください。また動詞について詳しく学習したい人は、Power Japanese シリーズ（講談社インターナシ

ョナル刊）の中に入っている『Japanese Verbs at a Glance』を参考にしてください。

　最近は日本国内だけではなく、世界各地の大きな都市で毎年日本語能力試験が行われています。この辞典には、初級から中級前半にかけて学習するすべての基本文型が載せられていますので、日本語能力試験の3級と4級を受験する人は効果的な準備ができると思います。

　この本が皆さんの日本語学習に役に立つよう願っております。終わりに、文型の辞典を書くように勧めてくださった編集担当のマイケル・ブレーズさんと鈴木重好さんに心から御礼を申しあげます。

ABBREVIATIONS AND DEFINITIONS

Adj = adjective, referring to both i-adjectives and na-adjectives

Adjective sentence = a sentence in which an adjective (i-adjective or na-adjective) comes at the end of the sentence and acts as the predicate (i.e., provides information about the subject).

Group 1 verb = a verb whose stem ends in a consonant; see Verb Conjugation Chart at back of book.

Group 2 verb = a verb whose stem ends in a vowel; see Verb Conjugation Chart at back of book.

Group 3 verb = an irregular verb; see Verb Conjugation Chart at back of book.

I-adj = i-adjective (an adjective that ends in "i" and directly precedes a noun: e.g., *ōkii* hito, "big person"); see Adjective Inflection Chart at back of book.

Interrog = an interrogative word ("who," "what," "where," etc.)

Na-adj = na-adjective (an adjective that has an irregular ending and is always followed by "na" when preceding a noun: e.g., *shizuka na hito*, "quiet person"); see Adjective Inflection Chart at back of book.

N = noun

Noun sentence = a sentence in which a noun comes at the end of the sentence and acts as the predicate)i.e., provides information about the subject).

Numbered abbreviations = numbers following abbreviations in formulas (*e.g., N1 wa N2 desu*) show the order of the parts of speech indicated by the abbreviations as well as the fact that abbreviations with different numbers represent different words for that part of speech.

V = verb (transitive and intransitive)

Verb sentence = a sentence in which a verb comes at the end of the sentence and acts as the predicate (i.e., provides information about the subject).

__ = underlined letters or words represent parts of speech that may be replaced by words of the same part of speech to create new sentences.

/ = a slash indicates that the word or words preceding it and the word or words following it represent alternative choices.

Noun and Adjective Sentences

This part of the dictionary covers seventeen patterns based on two of the three most fundamental types of Japanese sentence: the noun sentence and the adjective sentence. Noun sentences are sentences in which a noun comes at the end of the sentence and acts as the predicate (i.e., provides information about the subject). Adjective sentences are sentences in which an adjective comes as the end of the sentence and acts as the predicate.

Basic Patterns 1-3

CHAPTER 1

The first two patterns presented in this chapter represent the simplest form of two of the three most fundamental sentence types in the Japanese language: the noun sentence and the adjective sentence. Noun sentences are sentences in which a noun comes at the end of the sentence and acts as the predicate (i.e., provides information about the subject). Adjective sentences are sentences in which a adjective comes at the end of the sentence and acts as the predicate.

These two patterns (along with the *verb sentence* dealt with in Part 2) form the basis for any study of the language and, once learned, offer a powerful means of expressing oneself, even though the patterns themselves are quite easy. The third pattern taken up in this chapter represents an elaboration of the first two patterns, in which the subject of the sentence (a noun) is modified by an adjective.

Expressed in English terms, the three basic patterns are as follows:

Basic Pattern 1: **Noun is Noun**
"A dog is an animal."

Basic Pattern 2: **Noun is Adjective**
"A dog is loyal."

<u>Adjective Noun</u> is <u>Noun</u>
"A loyal dog is a friend."
or
<u>Adjective Noun</u> is <u>Adjective</u>
"A loyal dog is heartwarming."

The underlined words represent parts of speech, or slots, that can be filled by a word that is the same part of speech. In this way, the same pattern can be used to express many different things.

The three basic patterns will be taken up in order below, and then eight variations of these patterns will be introduced and exemplified. By the end of the chapter the student will be familiar with some of the most important ways of expressing oneself in Japanese.

Basic Pattern ① Noun Sentence

<u>N1</u> は <u>N2</u> です。	**私は田中です。**
N1 wa N2 desu.	*Watashi wa Tanaka desu.*
N1 is N2.	I am Mr. Tanaka.

This is one of the basic sentence patterns of the Japanese language. N1 is a noun and the subject of the sentence. N2 is a noun that provides information about N1. By substituting your own words for N1 and N2, you can create different sentences with this pattern, as we will show by example below.

This pattern may be represented in the following way:

Formula

N1 wa N2 desu.
N1 = a noun acting as a subject
N2 = a noun providing information about the subject

In this book two types of example sentences have been provided. One shows usage that is typical of polite occasions, and the other casual usage found among friends and family.

Polite

私は山田です。
Watashi wa Yamada desu.
I'm Mr. (or Ms.) Yamada.

私は日本人です。
Watashi wa Nihon-jin desu.
I'm a Japanese.

私は銀行員です。
Watashi wa ginkō-in desu.
I'm a bank employee.

As is clear from these examples, you can say many things about yourself (name, nationality, profession, etc.) by simply changing the second noun in the sentence.

Informal

BETWEEN MEN

山田：私、山田、よろしく。
Yamada: Watashi, Yamada. Yoroshiku.
Yamada: I'm Yamada. Nice to meet you.

田中：僕、田中。仕事は銀行員。
Tanaka: Boku, Tanaka. Shigoto wa ginkō-in.
Tanaka: I'm Tanaka, a bank employee.

Basic Pattern 2 Adj Sentence

N は **Adj** です。	私は若いです。
N wa Adj desu.	*Watashi wa wakai desu.*
N is Adj.	I'm young.

This is also a very basic pattern, in which N2 of Basic Pattern 1 has been replaced by an adjective. N is the subject, and the adjective gives information about that subject.

N wa Adj desu.
N = a noun acting as a subject
Adj = a na-adjective (na-adj) or i-adjective (i-adj) providing information about the subject

We can see from this that there are two different types of adjectives. The first type ends in an "i" and directly precedes a noun (e.g., *ōkii hito*, "big person"), while the second type has an irregular ending and is always followed by "na" when coming before a noun (e.g., *shizuka na hito*, "quiet person"). Adjectives of the first type are called i-adjectives, those of the second type na-adjectives. Some na-adjectives such as *kirei* ("beautiful) end with "i," but they do not conjugate in the way that i-adjectives do.

I-adjective examples

寒い *(samui)*   小さい *(chiisai)*

暑い *(atsui)*   広い *(hiroi)*

大きい *(ōkii)*   狭い *(semai)*

Na-adjective examples

綺麗 *(kirei)*   下手 *(heta)*

丈夫 *(jōbu)*   静か *(shizuka)*

上手 *(jōzu)*   簡単 *(kantan)*

For a list of adjective conjugations, see the Adjective Inflection Chart at the back of the book.

Basic Pattern 2 can be represented as follows:

$\underline{N}$ wa $\underline{Adj}$ desu.

N = a noun acting as a subject

Adj = a na-adjective or an i-adjective providing information about the subject

By placing various nouns into the first underlined slot and various adjectives into the second slot, you can make sentences expressing many different things. For example:

日本は小さいです。

Nihon wa chiisai desu.

Japan is small.

今東京は暑いです。

Ima Tōkyō wa atsui desu.

Tokyo is hot now.

山田さんは元気です。

Yamada-san wa genki desu.

Mr. (or Ms.) Yamada is well.

公園は静かです。

Kōen wa shizuka desu.

The park is quiet.

東京はにぎやかです。

Tōkyō wa nigiyaka desu.

Tokyo is lively.

BETWEEN WOMEN

久子：今日は暑いわね。
Hisako: Kyō wa atsui wa ne.
It's very hot today, isn't it.

友子：本当に暑いわね。
Tomoko: Hontō ni atsui wa ne.
Yes, it's very hot.

BETWEEN MEN

洋：山田君、元気？
Hiroshi: Yamada-kun, genki?
How's Yamada doing?

真：元気だよ。
Makoto: Genki da yo.
He's fine.

Pronouns such as *kore* (this), *sore* (that), and *are* (that over there) can be used in place of the noun acting as a subject. For example:

これは面白いです。
Kore wa omoshiroi desu.
This is interesting.

それは高いです。
Sore wa takai desu.
That is expensive.

あれは大きいです。
Are wa ōkii desu.
That over there is big.

1. **I-adj1 N1** は **N2 / I-adj2** です。
   I-adj1 N1 wa N2 / I-adj2 desu.
   Adj N is N / Adj.

   ## 白い建物は病院です。
   Shiroi tatemono wa byōin desu.
   The white building is a hospital.

   ## 大きい鞄は重いです。
   Ōkii kaban wa omoi desu.
   The big bag is heavy.

2. **Na-adj1 N1** は **N2 / Na-adj2** です。
   Na-adj1 N1 wa N2 / Na-adj2 desu.
   Adj N is N / Adj.

   ## 好きな食べ物はてんぷらです。
   Suki na tabemono wa tempura desu.
   My favorite food is tempura.

   ## 熱心な学生は武田さんです。
   Nesshin na gakusei wa Takeda-san desu.
   The hard-working student is Ms. Takeda.

As can be seen from the above, you can make a sentence longer and more informative by adding an adjective before the noun that is acting as the subject. This pattern can be represented by the following two formulas—one with an i-adjective preceding the noun acting as a subject and the other with a na-adjective preceding the noun acting as a subject. The predicate slot (the part providing information about the subject) can be either a noun or an adjective.

I-adjective Preceding a Noun

I-adj1 N1 wa N2 / I-adj2 desu.

I-adj1 = an i-adjective modifying a noun

N1 = a noun acting as a subject

N2 = a noun providing information about the subject

I-adj2 = an i-adjective providing information about the
subject

Polite

白い建物は病院です。

Shiroi tatemono wa byōin desu.

The white building is a hospital.

細い人は林さんです。

Hosoi hito wa Hayashi-san desu.

The slim man is Mr. Hayashi.

大きい鞄は重いです。

Ōkii kaban wa omoi desu.

The big bag is heavy.

Informal

BETWEEN MAN AND WOMEN

太郎：あの細い人、誰？

Tarō: Ano hosoi hito, dare?

Who is that, the slim person over there?

花子：林さんよ。

Hanako: Hayashi-san yo.

Mr. Hayashi.

As can be seen in the first part of this dialogue, *ano* (that over there) can preceed a combination of i-adjective plus noun. This also applies to na-adjectives and to the use of *sono* (that) and *kono* (this).

⟨Formula 2⟩

Na-adjective Preceding a Noun

Na-adj1 N1 wa N2 / Na-adj2 desu.

Na-adj1 = a na-adjective modifying a noun

N1 = a noun acting as a subject

N2 = a noun providing information about the subject

Na-adj2 = a na-adjective providing information about the subject

⟨Polite⟩

好きな食べ物はてんぷらです。

Suki na tabemono wa tempura desu.

My favorite food is tempura.

真っ白な花はばらです。

Masshiro na hana wa bara desu.

The pure white flower is a rose.

元気な子供は次郎です。

Genki na kodomo wa Jirō desu.

The lively child is Jiro.

⟨Informal⟩

BETWEEN TWO WOMEN

洋子：あの元気な子、次郎ちゃん？

Yōko: Ano genki na ko, Jirō-chan?

Is that lively boy Jiro?

春子：そう、次郎ちゃんはいつも元気ね。

Haruko: Sō, Jirō-chan wa itsumo genki ne.

Yes, Jiro is always lively.

In this section, we will look at some variations on the three basic patterns discussed above. Since these variations have a logic of their own, they will not be taken up strictly in the order of Basic Patterns 1, 2, and 3.

Variation ①　Noun Sentence with *mo* after Subject

N1 も N2 です。	**私も学生です。**
N1 mo N2 desu.	*Watashi mo gakusei desu.*
N1 also is N2.	I also am a student.

This is a variation of Basic Pattern 1 (*N1 wa N2 desu*) with the particle *mo*, which means "also" or "too," replacing *wa*. The pattern means "N1 is also N2," as we see below.

Formula

N1 mo N2 desu.

N1 = a noun acting as a subject

mo = a particle with the meaning of "also" or "too"

N2 = a noun providing information about the subject

Polite

私も日本人です。

Watashi mo Nihon-jin desu.

I also am a Japanese.

これもテレビです。

Kore mo terebi desu.

This also is a television.

BETWEEN MEN

林：これもテレビ？

Hayashi: Kore mo terebi?

This a TV too?

野村：それはパソコン。

Nomura: Sore wa pasokon.

That's a PC.

Variation **2** Adj Sentence with *mo* after Subject

N も **Adj** です。	今日も寒いです。
N mo Adj desu.	*Kyō mo samui desu.*
N also is Adj.	It's cold today also.

This is a variation of Basic Pattern 2 (<u>N</u> wa <u>Adj</u> desu), with *mo* replacing *wa*.

Formula

<u>N</u> *mo* <u>Adj</u> *desu.*

N = a noun acting as a subject

mo = a particle with the meaning of "also" or "too"

Adj = an i-adjective or na-adjective providing information about the subject

今日も寒いです。

Kyō mo samui desu.

It's cold today also.

この本も面白いです。

Kono hon mo omoshiroi desu.

This book also is interesting.

BETWEEN WOMEN

愛子：外、寒い？

Aiko: Soto, samui?

Is it cold outside?

幸子：今日も外は寒いわよ。

Sachiko: Kyō mo soto wa samui wa yo.

Yes, it's cold outside today too.

父も元気です。

Chichi mo genki desu.

My father is also fine.

ここも静かです。

Koko mo shizuka desu.

This place is also quiet.

BETWEEN WOMEN

緑：お母さん、お元気？
Midori: Okāsan, ogenki?
Is your mother well?

知子：ええ、お陰様で。父も元気よ。
Tomoko: Ee, okagesama de. Chichi mo genki yo.
Thank you, she's fine. My father too.

Variation **3** Noun Sentence in Past Tense

N1 は N2 でした。
N1 wa N2 deshita.
N1 was N2.

高橋さんは先生でした。
Takahashi-san wa sensei deshita.
Mr. Takahashi was a teacher.

This is a variation of Basic Pattern 1 (*N1 wa N2 desu*), with the present tense *desu* being changed into the past tense *deshita*. In other words, this variation is the past tense of Basic Pattern 1.

Formula

N1 wa N2 deshita.
N1 = a noun acting as a subject
N2 = a noun providing information about the subject
deshita = the past tense of *desu*

高橋さんは先生でした。

Takahashi-san wa sensei deshita.

Ms. Takahashi was a teacher.

あれは映画館でした。

Are wa eiga-kan deshita.

That over there was a movie theater.

BETWEEN WOMEN

弘子：あれは映画館だった？

Hiroko: Are wa eiga-kan datta?

Was that over there a movie theater?

秋子：違う、喫茶店だったわよ。

Akiko: Chigau, kissa-ten datta wa yo.

No, it was a tearoom (coffee shop).

Variation 4 I-adj/Na-adj Sentences in Past Tense

1. **N** は **I-adj** かった です。

   N wa I-adj (past tense) desu.

   N was Adj.

   昨日は寒かったです。

   Kinō wa samukatta desu.

   It was cold yesterday.

2. **N** は **Na-adj** でした。

   N wa Na-adj deshita.

   N was Adj.

富士山はきれいでした。

Fujisan wa kirei deshita.

Mt. Fuji was beautiful.

This is a variation of Basic Pattern 2 (*N wa Adj desu*) and involves changing the basic pattern from present to past tense. This variation has two parts because the past tenses of i-adjectives and na-adjectives are different. Let us first look at the formula for the past tense of an i-adjective.

Formula 1

Past Tense of an I-adjective

N wa I-adj (past tense) desu.

N = a noun acting as a subject

I-adj = an i-adjective providing information about the subject, in the past tense (see Adjective Inflection Chart for examples)

Polite

北海道は寒かったです。

Hokkaidō wa samukatta desu.

It was cold in Hokkaido.

お寿司はおいしかったです。

Osushi wa oishikatta desu.

The sushi was good.

映画は面白かったです。

Eiga wa omoshirokatta desu.

The movie was interesting.

BETWEEN WOMEN

宏美：そのリンゴ、甘かった？

Hiromi: Sono ringo, amakatta?

Was the apple sweet tasting?

美子：甘かったわよ。

Yoshiko; Amakatta wa yo.

Yes, it was.

Notice that the informal past tense involves nothing more than dropping *desu* from the polite pattern. Now let us look at the formula for the past tense of a na-adjective.

Formula 2

Past Tense of an Na-adjective

_N_ wa _Na-adj_ deshita.

N = a noun acting as a subject

Na-adj = a na-adjective providing information about the subject

deshita = the past tense of *desu*

Polite

東京はにぎやかでした。

Tōkyō wa nigiyaka deshita.

Tokyo was lively.

家族は元気でした。

Kazoku wa genki deshita.

My family were well.

それは丈夫でした。

Sore wa jōbu deshita.

It was sturdy (strong).

啓二：先生はとても親切だったよ。

Keiji: Sensei wa totemo shinsetsu datta yo.

The teacher was very kind.

孝：それは良かった。

Takashi: Sore wa yokatta.

That's nice.

Notice that in the informal pattern *deshita* becomes *datta*.

Variation 5 Noun/Adj Sentences as Questions

1. **N1** は **N2**ですか。

   N1 wa N2 desu ka.

   Is N1 N2?

   松本さんは外交官ですか。

   Matsumoto-san wa gaikō-kan desu ka.

   Is Mr. Matsumoto a diplomat?

2. **N** は **I-adj** ですか。

   N wa I-adj desu ka.

   Is N Adj?

   ハワイはあついですか。

   Hawai wa atsui desu ka.

   Is it warm in Hawaii?

3. **N** は **Na-adj** ですか。

   N wa Na-adj desu ka.

   Is N Adj?

> ## ご両親はお元気ですか。
> *Goryōshin wa ogenki desu ka.*
> Are your parents well?

This variation has three parts, all of which involve turning statements into questions. The first is based on Basic Pattern 1 (*N1 wa N2 desu*), and the next two on Basic Pattern 2 (*N wa Adj desu*). All three patterns, in polite usage, can be made into questions by adding *ka* at the end of the basic pattern. To create a question in the past tense using this pattern, substitute *deshita* for *desu*. The formula for the first part of this variation is:

Formula 1

Changing Basic Pattern 1 into a Question

N1 wa N2 desu ka.
N1 = a noun acting as a subject
N2 = a noun providing information about the subject
ka = a particle indicating a question

Polite

田中さんは銀行員ですか。
Tanaka-san wa ginkō-in desu ka.
Is Mr. Tanaka a bank employee?

井原：田中さんは先生ですか。
Ihara: Tanaka-san wa sensei desu ka.
Is Mrs. Tanaka a teacher?

古賀：はい、先生です。
Koga: Hai, sensei desu.
Yes, she is.

BETWEEN WOMEN

道子：田中さんは先生？
Michiko: Tanaka-san wa sensei?
Is Mr. Tanaka a teacher?

知美：そう、先生。
Tomomi: Sō, sensei.
Yes, he is.

The second part of this variation makes a question of a Basic Pattern 2 sentence (*N wa Adj desu*), in this case the adjective being an i-adjective.

Changing Basic Pattern 2 with I-adjective into a Question

*N wa **I-adj** desu ka.*
N = a noun acting as a subject
I-adj = an i-adjective providing information about the subject (in present or past tense)
ka = a particle indicating a question

佐藤: 北海道は今暑いですか。
Satō: Hokkaidō wa ima atsui desu ka.
Is it hot in Hokkaido now?

清水：はい、暑いです。
Shimizu: Hai, atsui desu.
Yes, it is.
or
清水：いいえ、寒いです。

Iie, samui desu.
No, it's cold.

BETWEEN MEN

佐藤：北海道、今暑い？
Satō: Hokkaidō, ima atsui?
Is it hot in Hokkaido now?

安井：うん、暑いよ。
Yasui: Un, atsui yo.
Yes, it is.

The third part of this variation makes a question of a Basic Pattern 2 sentence (*N* wa *Adj* desu), in this case the adjective being a na-adjective.

Formula 3

Changing Basic Pattern 2 with Na-adjective into a Question

N wa *Na-adj* desu ka?
N = a noun acting as a subject
N-adj = a na-adjective providing information about the subject (in present or past tense)
ka = a particle indicating a question

Polite

林さんは有名ですか。
Hayashi-san wa yūmei desu ka.
Is Mr. Hayashi famous?

公園は静かでしたか。
Kōen wa shizuka deshita ka.
Was the park quiet?

BETWEEN MEN

孝：これ、便利？
Takashi: Kore, benri?
Is this handy?

登：うん、便利だよ。
Noboru: Un, benri da yo.
Yes, it is.

Variation 6 · Questions with Interrogative Words

<u>N</u> は <u>Interrog</u> ですか。
N wa Interrog desu ka.
Interrog is N?

N はだれですか。
N wa dare desu ka.
Who is N?

N は何 ですか。
N wa nan desu ka.
What is N?

N はどこ (どちら) ですか。
N wa doko (dochira) desu ka.
Where is N?

This variation is based on Basic Pattern 1 (<u>*N1*</u> *wa* <u>*N2*</u> *desu*), but N2 is replaced by an interrogative word such as *nan* or *nani* (what), *ikutsu* (how many), *ikura* (how much), *ikaga* or *dō* (how), or *dōshite* or *naze* (why), and the sentence ends with *desu ka* (indicating a question in the present tense) or *deshita ka* (indicating a question in the past tense).

<u>N</u> wa <u>Interrog</u> desu ka.

N = a noun acting as a subject

Interrog = a word that asks a question about the subject

ka = a particle indicating a question

あの人はだれですか。

Ano hito wa dare desu ka.

Who is that person?

これは何ですか。

Kore wa nan desu ka.

What is this?

ここはどこですか。

Koko wa doko desu ka.

Where are we now? (lit., Where is this place?)

駅はどちらですか。

Eki wa dochira desu ka.

Where is the station?

BETWEEN WOMEN, LOOKING AT A PHOTO

長田：この人、誰？

Osada: Kono hito, dare?

Who is this (person)?

小川：私の姉よ。

Ogawa: Watashi no ane yo.

That's my big sister.

BETWEEN MEN

高橋：これは何だろう？

Takahashi: Kore wa nan darō?

What is this?

石田：鉄じゃないかな。

Ishida: Tetsu ja nai ka na.

I think it's iron.

BETWEEN WOMEN

知美：ここはどこ？

Tomomi: Koko wa doko?

Where are we now? (lit., Where is this place?)

光子：神谷町でしょう。

Mitsuko: Kamiyachō deshō.

It must be Kamiyachō.

宏子：駅はどっち？

Hiroko: Eki wa dotchi?

Where is the station?

純子：あそこ。

Sumiko: Asoko.

It's over there.

Variation **7** *N2 desu ka, N3 desu ka* as Predicate in Questions

1. <u>N1</u> は <u>N2</u> ですか、<u>N3</u>ですか。

   N1 wa N2 desu ka, N3 desu ka.

   Is N1 N2 or N3?

   田中さんは銀行員ですか、先生ですか。

> *Tanaka san wa ginkō-in desu ka, sensei desu ka.*
> Is Mr. Tanaka a bank employee or a teacher?

2. **N** は **Adj1** ですか、 **Adj2**ですか。
N wa Adj1 desu ka, Adj2 desu ka.
Is N Adj1 or Adj2?

このリンゴは甘いですか、すっぱいですか。
Kono ringo wa amai desu ka, suppai desu ka.
Is this apple sweet tasting or sour?

This variation can be seen as a modification of Variation 5 above, which itself is a variation of Basic Pattern 1 (*N1 wa N2 desu*) and Basic Pattern 2 (*N wa Adj desu*). It is used in asking questions that propose two alternatives. The same question can be made in the past tense by replacing *desu* with *deshita*.

Formula 1

N1 wa N2 desu ka, N3 desu ka.

N1 = a noun acting as a subject

N2, N3 = nouns potentially providing information about the subject, or in this case offering a choice of information about the subject

Polite

寺田：彼は中国人ですか、韓国人ですか。
Terada: Kare wa Chūgoku-jin desu ka, Kankoku-jin desu ka.
Is he a Chinese or a Korean?

石山：中国人です。
Ishiyama;: Chūgoku-jin desu.
He's a Chinese.

BETWEEN WOMEN

友子：彼女は中国人？　韓国人？
Tomoko: Kanojo wa Chūgoku-jin? Kankoku-jin?
Is she a Chinese or a Korean?

洋子：中国人よ。
Yōko: Chūgoku-jin yo.
She's a Chinese.

Here is the formula for the second type of variation, which is based on Basic Pattern 2 (*N wa Adj desu*). This type is itself divided into two since there are two types of adjectives, the i-adjective and the na-adjective.

Formula 2a

N wa I-adj1 desu ka, I-adj2 desu ka?

N = a noun acting as a subject

I-adj1, I-adj2 = i-adjectives potentially providing information about the subject, or in this case offering a choice of information about the subject

Polite

客：このりんごは甘いですか、すっぱいですか。
Kyaku: Kono ringo wa amai desu ka, suppai desu ka.
Customer: Is this apple sweet tasting or sour?

店員：甘いですよ。
Ten'in: Amai desu yo.
Clerk: It's sweet.

客：このりんごは甘い、すっぱい？

Kyaku: Kono ringo wa amai, suppai?

Customer: Is this apple sweet tasting or sour?

店員：甘いよ。

Ten'in: Amai yo.

Clerk: It's sweet.

Here is the formula for the second half of this variation, which is based on Basic Pattern 2 (*N wa Adj desu*) and deals with na-adjectives.

<u>N</u> wa <u>Na-adj1</u> desu ka, <u>Na-adj2</u> desu ka?

N = a noun acting as a subject

Na-adj1, Na-adj2 = na-adjectives potentially providing information about the subject, or in this case offering a choice of information

富田：交通機関は便利ですか、不便ですか。

Tomita: Kōtsū-kikan wa benri desu ka, fuben desu ka.

Is the transportation convenient or inconvenient?

野本：とても不便です。

Nomoto: Totemo fuben desu.

It's very inconvenient.

Variation ⑧ Negative Noun/Adj Sentences

1. <u>N1</u> は <u>N2</u> ではありません /
   ではありませんでした。

N1 wa N2 dewa arimasen / dewa arimasen deshita.
N1 is / was not N2.

私は中国人ではありません。

Watashi wa Chūgoku-jin dewa arimasen.
I'm not a Chinese.

2. **N** は **I-adj** くない / くなかったです。

N wa I-adj-ku nai / -ku nakatta desu.
N1 is / was not Adj.

これは高くなかったです。

Kore wa takaku nakatta desu.
This wasn't expensive.

3. **N** は **Na-adj** ではありません /
ではありませんでした。

N wa Na-adj dewa arimasen /
 dewa arimasen deshita.
N is / was not Adj.

景色はきれいではありませんでした。

Keshiki wa kirei dewa arimasen deshita.
The view wasn't beautiful.

This variation is based on Basic Pattern 1 (*N1 wa N2 desu*) and Basic Pattern 2 (*N wa Adj desu*, in both its i-adjective and na-adjective forms). In all three cases, the positive statement given in the basic patterns is turned into a negative one, in both the present and past tenses. *Dewa arimasen* can be replaced by *ja arimasen*, which is more casual and slightly more emphatic. First is the variation based on Basic Pattern 1.

Negative Noun Sentence

N1 wa *N2* dewa arimasen / dewa arimasen deshita.

N1 = a noun acting as a subject

N2 = a noun providing information about the subject

dewa arimasen = negative form of *aru* in the present tense

dewa arimasen deshita = negative form of *aru* in the past tense

Polite

私は中国人ではありません。

Watashi wa Chūgoku-jin dewa arimasen.

I'm not a Chinese.

私は日本人ではありません。

Watashi wa Nihon-jin dewa arimasen.

I'm not a Japanese.

私は銀行員じゃありません。

Watashi wa ginkō-in ja arimasen.

I'm not a bank employee.

Informal

BETWEEN A MAN (TANAKA) AND A WOMAN (YAMADA)

田中：君も銀行員？

Tanaka: Kimi mo ginkō-in?

Tanaka: Are you a bank employee too?

山田：私、銀行員じゃないわ。

Yamada: Watashi, ginkō-in ja nai wa.

No, I'm not a bank employee.

Note that the informal version of *dewa arimasen* is *ja nai.*

Here is the first of the two variations based on Basic

Pattern 2 (*N wa Adj desu*), in which an i-adjective appears in the negative form.

Formula 2

Negative I-adjective Sentence

*N wa **I-adj-ku nai desu / -ku nakatta desu**.*

N = a noun acting as a subject

I-adj-*ku nai* = the negative form of an i-adjective in the present tense

I-adj-*ku nakatta* = the negative form of an i-adjective in the past tense

Polite

今日は寒くないです。

Kyō wa samuku nai desu.
It's not cold today.

東京は暑くなかったです。

Tōkyō wa atsuku nakatta desu.
It wasn't warm in Tokyo.

Informal

山田：今、北海道は寒い？

Yamada: Ima, Hokkaidō wa samui?
Ms. Yamada: Is it cold in Hokkaido now?

田中：いや、北海道は今寒くないよ。

Tanaka: Iya, Hokkaidō wa ima samuku nai yo.
Mr. Tanaka: No, it isn't cold in Hokkaido now.

城山：このパソコン、高かった？

Shiroyama: Kono pasokon, takakatta?
Was this PC expensive?

高見：いや、高くなかったよ。

Takami: Iya, takaku nakatta yo.

No, it wasn't expensive.

Here is the second of the two variations based on Basic Pattern 2 (*N wa Adj desu*), in which a na-adjective appears in the negative form. The formula is:

Formula 3

Negative Na-adjective Sentence

<u>N</u> wa <u>Na-adj</u> dewa arimasen / dewa arimasen deshita.

N = a noun acting as a subject

Na-adj = a na-adjective providing information about the subject

dewa arimasen = negative form of the verb *aru* in the present tense

dewa arimasen deshita = negative form of the verb *aru* in the past tense

Polite

この花はあまりきれいではありません。

Kono hana wa amari kirei dewa arimasen.

These flowers are not very pretty.

あの人は親切じゃありませんでした。

Ano hito wa shinsetsu ja arimasen deshita.

That person was not kind.

Informal

BETWEEN WOMEN

雪子：あの歌手、有名？

Yukiko: Ano kashu, yūmei?

Is that singer famous?

光子：まだ有名じゃないわ。

Mitsuko: Mada yūmei ja nai wa.

No, he isn't famous yet.

Basic Patterns 4-5

In this chapter we look at two basic patterns in which the subject is a noun and the predicate (the part providing information about the noun) is a combination of two nouns. In Basic Pattern 4, this combination consists of one noun modifying the other. In Basic Pattern 5, the combination consists of two parallel nouns.

In English these patterns might be represented as follows:

Basic Pattern 4: **Noun is Noun's Noun.**
> A dog is man's friend.
> (or, Dogs are friends of man.)

Basic Pattern 5: **Noun is Noun and Noun.**
> A dog is a friend and a companion.

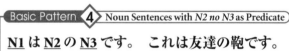

Basic Pattern **4** Noun Sentences with *N2 no N3* as Predicate

N1 は N2 の N3 です。   これは友達の鞄です。

N1 wa N2 no N3 desu.   *Kore wa tomodachi no kaban desu.*

N1 is N2's N3.   This is a friend's bag.

In this pattern, the predicate has become longer and more complicated by placing the particle *no* between two nouns. The particle indicates that N2 modifies N3. This pattern can indicate possession (a friend's bag), location (the bag on the table), material (a leather bag), and more. (For more information about *no*, see my *All about Particles*.) When the sentence expresses possession, N2 indicates the possessor and N3 the thing possessed. In questions, N2 is an interrogative word such as *dare* (who), *dore* (which), or *doko* (where).

Formula

<u>N1</u> *wa* <u>N2</u> *no* <u>N3</u> *desu.*
N1 = a noun acting as a subject
N2 = a noun modifying a following noun
N3 = a noun (with its modifier) providing information about the subject
no = a particle indicating that N2 modifies N3

▮ Possession

Polite

宮田：これは誰の鞄ですか。
Miyata: Kore wa dare no kaban desu ka.
Whose bag is this?

森下：それは社長の鞄です。
Morishita: Sore wa shachō no kaban desu.
That's the president's bag.

BETWEEN MEN

宮田：これ、だれの鞄？

Miyata: Kore, dare no kaban?

Whose bag is this?

森下：それ社長の鞄。

Morishita: Sore shachō no kaban.

That's the president's bag.

2 Apposition

あの方は社長の佐藤さんです。

Ano kata wa shachō no Satō-san desu.

That person is the president, Mrs. Sato.

彼は会社の同僚の田中です。

Kare wa kaisha no dōryō no Tanaka desu.

He is Mr. Tanaka, one of my colleagues.

3 Materials

これは木の靴です。

Kore wa ki no kutsu desu.

These are wooden shoes.

あれは竹のかごです。

Are wa take no kago desu.

That one over there is a bamboo basket.

4 Origin

山本さんの車はイタリアの車です。

Yamamoto-san no kuruma wa Itaria no kuruma desu.

Mr. Yamamoto's car is Italian.

これはスイスのチョコレートです。
Kore wa Suisu no chokorēto desu.
This is Swiss chocolate.

As the first example sentence under "Origin" shows, you can also use the N *no* N formula for the subject, resulting in the pattern *N1 no N2 wa N3 no N4 desu.*

5 Location

机の下
tsukue no shita
under the desk

机の上
tsukue no ue
on the desk

箱の中
hako no naka
in (inside) the box

私の家の前は区の公園です。
Watashi no uchi no mae wa ku no kōen desu.
In front of my house there is a ward park.

6 Kind, Type, Category

これは私のドイツ語の辞書です。
Kore wa watashi no Doitsu-go no jisho desu.
This is my German dictionary.

原：山田さんは何の先生ですか？
Hara: Yamada-san wa nan no sensei desu ka?
What does Mr. Yamada teach?

宇野：スペイン語の先生です。

Uno: Supein-go no sensei desu.

He teaches Spanish.

| Variation ▷ 1 | Noun Sentence with *N2 no* as Predicate |

N1 は **N2** のです。　　これは私のです。

N1 wa N2 no desu.　　*Kore wa watashi no desu.*

N1 is N2's.　　　　　　This is mine.

This is a variation of Basic Pattern 4 (*N1 wa N2 no N3 desu*). If N3 is understood by all parties to a conversation, it is not expressed. N2 is still a modifier, in this case of *no*, which functions as a sort of pronoun, designating something that has been previously talked about or is understood from context. A similar situation can be found in the English sentences "This is my book" and "This is mine," where "mine" means "the book belonging to me."

Formula

N1 wa N2 no desu.

N1 = a noun acting as a subject

N2 = a noun modifying *no*

no = a particle indicating that one noun modifies another; in this case, the second noun is understood and therefore not expressed

Polite

富田：これは誰の傘ですか。

Tomita: Kore wa dare no kasa desu ka.

Whose umbrella is this?

山下：それは私のです。

Yamashita: Sore wa watashi no desu.

That's mine.

BETWEEN WOMEN

富田：これ、だれの傘？

Tomita: Kore, dare no kasa?

Whose umbrella is this?

山下：私の。

Yamashita: Watashi no.

It's mine.

Instead of a noun preceding *no* (<u>N1</u> *wa* <u>N2</u> *no desu*), an i-adjective can preceed it (<u>N1</u> *wa* <u>I-adj</u> *no desu*).

これは大きいのです。

Kore wa ōkii no desu.

This is a big one.

Here are some examples of short phrases with *no* following an adjective:

赤いの

akai no

red one

古いの

furui no

old one

長いの

nagai no

long one

面白いの

omoshiroi no

interesting one

重いの

omoi no

heavy one

1. <u>N1</u> の <u>N2</u> は <u>N3</u> です。

   N1 no N2 wa N3 desu.
   N1's N2 is N3.

   私の傘はそれです。

   Watashi no kasa wa sore desu.
   My umbrella is that one.

2. <u>N1</u> の <u>N2</u> は <u>Adj</u> です。

   N1 no N2 wa Adj desu.
   N1's N2 is Adj.

   富士山の頂上は寒いです。

   Fujisan no chōjō wa samui desu.
   The summit of Mt. Fuji is cold.

   あの俳優の顔はハンサムです。

   Ano haiyu no kao wa hansamu desu.
   That actor's face is handsome.

These are variations of Basic Pattern 4 (<u>*N1 wa N2 no N3 desu*</u>), with the positions of N1 and <u>*N2 no N3*</u> reversed in the first variation, and in the second variation the same reversal taking place with N1 being further replaced by an adjective (either na-adjective or i-adjective).

Formula 1

<u>*N1 no N2 wa N3 desu.*</u>
N1 = a noun modifying a following noun
N2 = a noun acting as a subject
N3 = a noun providing information about the subject

久子さんの靴は茶色です。

Hisako-san no kutsu wa chairo desu.
Ms. Hisako's shoes are brown.

Note here that *chairo* is a noun; the adjective is *chairoi*.

武田さんの事務所は3階です。

Takeda-san no jimusho wa sangai desu.
Mr. Takeda's office is on the third floor.

Informal

BETWEEN WOMEN

貞子：あなたの時計、スイス製？

Sadako: Anata no tokei, Suisu-sei?
Is your watch Swiss-made?

竜子：ううん、日本製よ。

Tatsuko: Uun, Nihon-sei yo.
No, it was made in Japan.

Formula 2

N1 no N2 wa Adj desu.

N1 = a noun modifying a following noun
N2 = a noun acting as a subject
Adj = an i-adjective or na-adjective giving information
about the subject

Polite

あの子の頬は赤いです。

Ano ko no hoho wa akai desu.
The child's cheeks are red.

この機械の操作は簡単です。

Kono kikai no sōsa wa kantan desu.

The operation of this machine is simple.

街のオペラハウスは立派でした。

Machi no opera-hausu wa rippa deshita.

The city's opera house was impressive.

Informal

BETWEEN WOMEN

雪子：あなたの新しいドレス、赤いの？

Yukiko: Anata no atarashii doresu, akai no?

Is your new dress red?

Notice in the above example that there is an i-adjective preceding N2.

Informal

BETWEEN MEN

孝夫：来週の週末、暇？

Takao: Raishū no shūmatsu, hima?

Are you free next weekend?

達彦：うん、暇だけど。

Tatsuhiko: Un, hima da kedo.

Well, yes, I am free.

Basic Pattern **5** Noun Sentence with *N2 to N3* as Predicate

<u>N1</u> は <u>N2</u> と <u>N3</u> です。

N1 wa N2 to N3 desu.

N1 is N2 and N3.

外国人はアメリカ人とフランス人です。

Gaikoku-jin wa Amerika-jin to Furansu-jin desu.

The foreigners are Americans and French.

In this pattern, the subject is a single noun, and the predicate consists of two nouns joined by the conjunction *to* ("and").

Formula

N1 wa N2 to N3 desu.

N1 = a noun acting as a subject

N2 = a noun (acting in conjunction with N3) providing information about the subject

N3 = a noun (acting in conjunction with N2) providing information about the subject

to = a particle connecting N2 and N3

Polite

学生は中島さんと武藤さんです。

Gakusei wa Nakajima-san to Mutō-san desu.

The students are Nakajima and Muto.

私の本はこれとそれです。

Watashi no hon wa kore to sore desu.

My books are this one and that one.

白い花はバラとチューリップです。

Shiroi hana wa bara to chūrippu desu.

The white flowers are roses and tulips.

神谷：小池さんの本はどれ？
Kamiya: Koike-san no hon wa dore?
Which books are yours, Koike?

小池：これとそれ。
Koike: Kore to sore.
This one and that one.

Variation **1** Noun/Adj Sentence with *N1 to N2* as Subject

1. <u>N1</u> と <u>N2</u> は <u>N3</u> です。
   N1 to N2 wa N3 desu.
   N1 and N2 are N3.

   鳥居さんと杉田さんは会社員です。
   Torii-san to Sugita-san wa kaisha-in desu.
   Mr. Torii and Mr. Sugita are office workers (company employees).

2. <u>N1</u> と <u>N2</u> は <u>Adj</u> です。
   N1 to N2 wa Adj desu.
   N1 and N2 are Adj.

   寿司とてんぷらはおいしかったです。
   Sushi to tempura wa oishikatta desu.
   The sushi and tempura were delicious.

   波と風は穏やかです。
   Nami to kaze wa odayaka desu.
   The waves and the wind are calm.

In the first part of this variation on Basic Pattern 5 (*N1 wa N2 to N3 desu*), the single noun and the two connected nouns have reversed positions, making it possible to create a more complicated subject; in the second part, the noun providing information about the subject is replaced by an adjective.

Formula 1

N1 to N2 wa N3 desu.
N1 = a noun (in conjunction with N2) acting as a subject
N2 = a noun (in conjunction with N1) acting as a subject
to = a particle connecting N1 and N2
N3 = a noun providing information about the subject

Polite

岸さんと鈴木さんは政治家です。
Kishi-san to Suzuki-san wa seiji-ka desu.
Mr. Kishi and Mr. Suzuki are politicians.

その車とこの車は外国製です。
Sono kuruma to kono kuruma wa gaikoku-sei desu.
This car and that car are foreign-made.

Informal

BETWEEN COLLEAGUES

沢田：今年はどの銀行が赤字？
Sawada: Kotoshi wa dono ginkō ga akaji?
Which banks are in the red this year?

久保：A銀行とD銀行が赤字らしいね。
Kubo: A ginkō to D ginkō ga akaji rashii ne.
A bank and D bank are apparently in the red.

N1 to N2 wa Adj desu.

N1 = a noun (in conjunction with N2) acting as a subject

N2 = a noun (in conjunction with N1) acting as a subject

to = a particle connecting N1 and N2

Adj = an i-adjective or na-adjective providing information
about the subject

Polite

東京と横浜は今晩寒いでしょう。

Tōkyō to Yokohama wa konban samui deshō.

Tokyo and Yokohama will be cold tonight.

森：どんな作曲家が好きですか？

Mori: Donna sakkyoku-ka ga suki desu ka?

Which (what kind of) composers do you like?

秦：モーツァルトとショパンが好きです。

Hata: Mōtsuaruto to Shopan ga suki desu.

I like Mozart and Chopin.

Informal

BETWEEN WOMEN

内海：誰と誰が熱心？

Utsumi: Dare to dare ga nesshin?

Who's enthusiastic?

太田：後藤さんと今井さん。

Ōta: Gotō-san to Imai-san.

Ms. Goto and Ms. Imai.

<u>N1</u> は <u>N2</u> で、<u>N3</u> は <u>N4</u> です。

N1 wa N2 de, N3 wa N4 desu.

N1 is N2, and N3 is N4.

トムさんはアメリカ人で、伊藤さんは日本人 です。

Tomu-san wa Amerika-jin de, Itō-san wa Nihon-jin desu.

Tom is an American, and Ito is a Japanese.

これはフランス語の本で、それはドイツ語の 本です。

Kore wa Furansu-go no hon de, sore wa Doitsu-go no hon desu.

This is a French book, and that is a German book.

This pattern shows how to connect two noun sentences (Basic Pattern 1: *N1 wa N2 desu*). This can be done by forming two Basic Pattern 1 sentences one after the other and dropping *su* from *desu* at the end of the first sentence. If this newly formed sentence ends in *desu*, then both parts of the sentence are in the present tense. If it ends in *deshita*, then both parts of the sentence are in the past tense. Since the new sentence is formed from two independent sentences, it is called a compound sentence.

Formula

N1 wa N2 de, N3 wa N4 desu.

N1 = a noun acting as the subject of the first part of the compound sentence

N2 = a noun providing information about N1

de = a conjunctive form of *desu*

N3 = a noun acting as the subject of the second part of the compound sentence

N4 = a noun providing information about N3

Polite

ここは外務省で、そこは大蔵省です。

Koko wa Gaimu-shō de, soko wa Ōkura-shō desu.

This is the Foreign Ministry, and that is the Finance Ministry.

白いのはバラで、赤いのは椿です。

Shiroi no wa bara de, akai no wa tsubaki desu.

The white one is a rose, and the red one is a camellia.

Informal

BETWEEN MEN

菊池：今井君と小沼君の週末の予定、知ってる？

Kikuchi: Imai-kun to Onuma-kun no shūmatsu no yotei shitte 'ru?

Do you know Imai's and Onuma's plans for this weekend?

川口：今井君はスキーで、小沼君はゴルフだって。

Kawaguchi: Imai-kun wa sukī de, Onuma-kun wa gorufu datte.

Imai's going skiing, and Onuma's playing golf, I hear.

N は **Adj1** て / で **Adj2** です。

N wa Adj1 -te / de Adj2 desu.

N is Adj1 and Adj2.

寮は広くて、明るいです。

Ryō wa hirokute, akarui desu.

The dormitory is big and sunny.

子供は元気で可愛いです。

Kodomo wa genki de kawaii desu.

The children are full of energy and cute.

This is a variation of Basic Pattern 2 (*N wa Adj desu*), but in this case the single adjective becomes two adjectives. In order to combine two adjectives in this way, the first adjective must appear in its *te* form if it is an i-adjective, or if it is a na-adjective, be followed by *de*. The last adjective retains its regular form. If three adjectives appear in succession (and this number should be seen as a maximum), then the first two appear in *te* or *de* forms and the last in its regular form. Here are two examples of adjectival changes with three adjectives in a row.

I-adjectives

白い、大きい、高い → 白くて、大きくて高いです

shiroi, ōkii, takai → Shirokute, ōkikute takai desu.

Na-adjectives

きれい、丈夫、静か → きれいで、丈夫で、静かです

kirei, jōbu, shizuka → Kirei de, jōbu de, shizuka desu.

When two or three adjectives are aligned in this way, they should all be either positive or negative in meaning, not a mixture of the two, which would call for another sentence pattern. In the following two sentences, the first shows a positive bent, the second a negative one.

この家は、大きくて、新しくて、きれいです。

Kono uchi wa, ōkikute, atarashikute, kirei desu.

This house is big, new, and clean.

この家は、小さくて、ふるくて、きたないです。

Kono uchi wa, chiisakute, furukute, kitanai desu.

This house is small, old, and dirty.

Here is an unacceptable example that mixes the positive and negative.

この家は小さくて、新しくて、高いです。

Kono uchi wa chiisakute, atarashikute, takai desu.

This house is small, new, and expensive.

For one way of expressing this type of mixture, see Basic Pattern 8 in Chapter 3.

─────────────────────────────────────

◖Formula▸

N wa Adj1 -te / de Adj2 desu.

N = a noun acting as a subject

Adj1 = an i-adjective (in its *te* form) or a na-adjective (followed by *de*) that provides information about the subject

Adj2 = an i-adjective or a na-adjective providing information about the subject

あのレストランは安くて、おいしいです。

Ano resutoran wa yasukute, oishii desu.
That restaurant is cheap and delicious.

地球は青くて、きれいです。

Chikyū wa aokute, kirei desu.
The earth is blue and beautiful.

この靴は丈夫で、はきやすいです。

Kono kutsu wa jōbu de, hakiyasui desu.
These shoes are sturdy and comfortable (easy to wear).

Informal

BETWEEN WOMEN

神谷：旅行、どうだった？

Kamiya: Ryokō, dō datta?
How was the trip?

江口：楽しくて、すばらしかったわ。

Eguchi: Tanoshikute, subarashikatta wa.
It was great and a lot of fun.

Variation 4 Adj Sentences with Adj Connected by *shi/da shi*

<u>N</u> は <u>Adj1</u> し / だし、<u>Adj2</u> です。

N wa Adj1 shi / da shi, Adj2 desu.
N is Adj1 and also Adj2.

寮は広いし、明るいです。

Ryō wa hiroi shi, akarui desu.
The dormitory is big and sunny as well.

> ## ゆり子は元気だし、きれいです。
> *Yuriko wa genki da shi, kirei desu.*
> Yuriko is full of pep and pretty as well.

This variation has almost the same meaning as Variation 3 above. But whereas the *te* or *de* connection always contains the possibility of a cause and effect relationship between the two adjectives, the *shi* / *da shi* connection presents the two adjectives as independent attributes without any causal relationship. The adjectives used together should be similar in positive or negative nuance.

Formula

N wa Adj1 shi / da shi Adj2 desu.

N = a noun acting as a subject

Adj1 = an i-adjective (followed by *shi*) or a na-adjective (followed by *da shi*) providing information about the subject

Adj2 = an i-adjective or na-adjective in its regular form providing information about the subject

Polite

あのレストランは安いし、おいしいです。
Ano resutoran wa yasui shi, oishii desu.
That restaurant is cheap and delicious as well.

杉本さんのマンションは高いし、駅から遠いです。
Sugimoto-san no manshon wa takai shi, eki kara tōi desu.
Mr. Sugimoto's apartment is expensive and far from the station as well.

BETWEEN WOMEN

京子：新しいパソコン、いい？

Kyōko: Atarashii pasokon, ii?

Is your new PC OK?

良子：軽いし、使いやすいわよ。

Yoshiko: Karui shi, tsukaiyasui wa yo.

Yes, it is light and easy to use as well.

Basic Patterns 6-14

In this chapter we see a complication of both the subject and and the predicate (the part of the sentence giving information about the subject of the sentence). Patterns containing both topics (followed by *wa*) and subjects (followed by *ga*) are also introduced.

Basic Pattern 6 Adj Sentence with Topic (*wa*) and Subject (*ga*)

<u>N1</u> は <u>N2</u> が <u>Adj</u> です。   **象は鼻が長いです。**
N1 wa N2 ga Adj desu.   *Zō wa hana ga nagai desu.*
Concerning N1, N2 is Adj.   Elephants have long noses.

In this pattern, we encounter *wa* as marking the topic of a sentence and *ga* as marking the subject (see my *All about Particles* for more information about *wa* and *ga*). Literally we might translate the example sentence above as follows: "As for the elephant (topic), its nose (subject) is long." In this pattern, *N2 ga Adj desu* gives information about the topic, concerning its attributes, condition, situation, or state of being. According to the context, the topic may not be mentioned at all—e.g., A: "What do you think about elephants?" B: "They have rather long noses." When this pattern is translated into English, the topic often becomes the subject of the sentence.

_N1_ wa _N2_ ga _Adj_ desu.

N1 = a noun acting as the topic of a sentence
N2 = a noun acting as the subject of the sentence
Adj = an i-adjective or na-adjective giving information about the subject of the sentence

竹子さんは目が大きいです。

Takeko-san wa me ga ōkii desu.
Takeko has big eyes.

東京は人が多いです。

Tōkyō wa hito ga ōi desu.
Tokyo has many people.

BETWEEN WOMEN

榎本：成田空港は交通が不便ね。

Enomoto: Narita kūkō wa kōtsū ga fuben ne.
Getting out to Narita airport is a hassle, isn't it.

市川：それに交通費も高いわね。

Ichikawa: Sore ni kōtsū-hi mo takai wa ne.
Besides that, the transportation fare is so high.

<u>N1</u> は <u>N2</u> も <u>Adj1</u> し／だし <u>N3</u> も <u>Adj2</u> です。

N1 wa N2 mo Adj1 shi / da shi N3 mo Adj2 desu.

Concerning N1, N2 is Adj1, and N3 is Adj2.

松本さんは頭もいいし、体も丈夫です。

Matsumoto-san wa atama mo ii shi, karada mo jōbu desu.

Mr. Matsumoto is smart and sound of body.

This pattern is similar to Basic Pattern 6 (*<u>N1</u> wa <u>N2</u> ga <u>Adj</u> desu*), but here the topic is followed by a compound sentence in parallel construction. The parallelism is achieved not only by the fact that the two parts of the compound sentence have an N plus Adj construction, but by the fact that the two parts are connected by *shi* and each noun acting as a subject is followed by *mo* ("also"). The two adjectives connected by *shi / da shi* are different from those connected by *-te / de* in Basic Pattern 5, Variation 3 (*<u>N</u> wa <u>Adj1</u> -te / de <u>Adj2</u> desu*) in that they are presented as independent attributes, whereas those in the latter always contain the possibility of a casual relationship. These attributes should share some common element, not be of random nature or contrary in meaning. For a means of presenting contrasting points, see Basic Pattern 8 (*<u>N1</u> wa <u>N2</u> wa <u>Adj1</u> ga / da ga, <u>N3</u> wa <u>Adj2</u> desu*).

***

Formula

<u>N1</u> wa <u>N2</u> mo <u>Adj1</u> shi / da shi <u>N3</u> mo <u>Adj2</u> desu.

N1 = the topic of the sentence

N2 = a noun acting as the subject of the first part of the compound sentence

mo = a particle meaning "also"

Adj1 = an i-adjective or na-adjective providing information about the subject (N2) of the first part of the compound sentence *shi* = a particle that follows i-adjectives (in their regular form) and na-adjectives (followed by *da*) to indicate that more information will follow in sentence form

N3 = a noun acting as the subject of the second part of the compound sentence

Adj2 = an i-adjective or na-adjective providing information about the subject (N3) of the second part of the compound sentence

Polite

あの会社は資金も充分だし、人材も多いです。

Ano kaisha wa shikin mo jūbun da shi, jinzai mo ōi desu.

That company has ample funds as well as many capable people.

このホテルは値段も安いし、設備もいいです。

Kono hoteru wa nedan mo yasui shi, setsubi mo ii desu.

This hotel is inexpensive and also has good facilities.

Informal

BETWEEN MEN

野田：山登りはどうだった？

Noda: Yama-nobori wa dō datta?

How was the mountain climbing?

遠藤：天気も良かったし、景色もすばらしかったよ。

Endō: Tenki mo yokatta shi, keshiki mo subarashikatta yo.

The weather was fine, and the scenery was just wonderful.

Informal

BETWEEN WOMEN

栗原：この茶碗、きれいね。

Kurihara: Kono chawan kirei ne.

This tea bowl is pretty, isn't it.

北川：そう、形もいいし、色も鮮やかね。

Kitagawa: Sō, katachi mo ii shi, iro mo azayaka ne.

You're right. The shape is good, and the color is brilliant.

Basic Pattern 8 — **Adj Sentences Connected by *ga/da ga***

<u>N1</u> は <u>N2</u> は <u>Adj1</u> が / だが <u>N3</u> は <u>Adj2</u> です。

N1 wa N2 wa Adj1 ga / da ga N3 wa Adj2 desu.

Concerning N1, N2 is Adj1, but N3 is Adj2.

松本さんは頭はいいが、体は弱いです。

Matsumoto-san wa atama wa ii ga, karada wa yowai desu.

Mr. Matsumoto is smart but not physically strong.

In this pattern two sentences, connected by *ga* ("but"), stand in contrast to one another. Not only is the topic followed by *wa*, but the subjects of the two sentences are followed by *wa*, indicating that they are being contrasted. For a means of connecting two sentences that present similar information, see Basic Pattern 7 (*<u>N1</u> wa <u>N2</u> mo <u>Adi1</u> shi / da shi <u>N3</u> mo <u>Adj2</u> desu*).

Formula

<u>N1</u> wa <u>N2</u> wa <u>Adj1</u> ga / da ga, <u>N3</u> wa <u>Adj2</u> desu.

N1 = the topic of the sentence

N2 = a noun acting as the subject of the first part of the compound sentence

Adj1 = an i-adjective or na-adjective giving information about the subject (N2) of the first part of the compound sentence

ga = a conjunction ("but") following an i-adjective or a na-adjective with *da*

N3 = a noun acting as the subject of the second part of the compound sentence

Adj2 = an i-adjective or na-adjective providing information about the subject (N3) of the second part of the compound sentence

カナダは夏はすばらしいが、冬は大変寒いです。

Kanada wa natsu wa subarashii ga, fuyu wa taihen samui desu.

In Canada, summer is wonderful, but winter is very cold.

川村さんは歌は上手ですが、ピアノはだめです。

Kawamura-san wa uta wa jōzu desu ga, piano wa dame desu.

Mr. Kawamura is good at singing, but poor at the piano.

BETWEEN GIRL STUDENTS

康子：あなた、数学良くできるわね。

Yasuko: Anata, sūgaku yoku dekiru wa ne.

You are so good at math, aren't you.

明美：数学は好きなんだけど、英語はぜんぜんうまくないの。

Akemi: Sūgaku wa suki nan da kedo, Eigo wa zenzen umaku nai no.

I like math, but my English is really bad.

Basic Pattern **9** Adj Sentences Connected by *te/de*

<u>N1</u> は <u>Adj1</u> て / で (<u>N2</u> は) <u>Adj2</u> です。

N1 wa Adj1 -te / de (N2 wa) Adj2 desu.

N1 is Adj1, and / so N2 is Adj2.

景色がよくて、（私たちは）楽しいです。

Keshiki ga yokute, (watashi-tachi wa) tanoshii desu.

The scenery is nice, and we're enjoying ourselves.

庭は広くて（私達は）気持ちいいです。

Niwa wa hirokute (watashi-tachi wa) kimochi ii desu.

The garden is big, so we feel good.

In this pattern, two parts of a compound sentence make similiarly positive or negative statements about the same or different topics. The connection between the two parts is made with the *te* form of an i-adjective or the *de* form of a na-adjective, which are both essentially neutral and would normally be interpreted as "and." However, if the relationship between the two parts seems to be clearly one of cause and effect, then the connecting *te* and *de* might be translated as "so." The same type of thing can be found in English: e.g., "I had a headache and went to bed," where cause and effect is clear, and the conjuction could be "so" just as well as "and." In the formula for this pattern, N2, which indicates the subject of the second part of the sentence, is often omitted if the same as the first part or understood from context.

◖Formula ▶──────────────

N1 wa Adj1 -te / de (N2 wa) Adj2 desu.

N1 = a noun acting as the subject of the the first part of the sentence

Adj1 = an i-adjective or na-adjective providing information about the subject N1

te = the *te*-form of an i-adjective, connecting the first half of the sentence to the second

N2 = a noun acting as the subject of the second part of the sentence

Adj2 = an i-adjective or na-adjective providing information about the subject N2

Polite

この家は、小さくて、住みにくいです。

Kono uchi wa chiisakute, suminikui desu.

This house is small and hard to live in.

この料理は甘すぎて、おいしくないです。

Kono ryōri wa amasugite, oishiku nai desu.

This food is too sweet and doesn't taste good.

Informal

BETWEEN MEN

金子：この頃何か面白い本読んだ？

Kaneko: Kono goro nanika omoshiroi hon yonda?

Have you read any interesting books recently?

小笠原：忙しくて、全然 だめ。

Ogasawara: Isogashikute, zenzen dame.

I'm too busy to read.

Informal

BETWEEN WOMEN

小林：しばらくね。元気？

Kobayashi: Shibaraku ne. Genki?

It's been a while. How are you?

沢井：それが、頭と喉が痛くて、（私は）元気 じゃないの。

Sawai: Sorega, atama to nodo ga itakute, (watashi wa) genki ja nai no.

The truth is, my head hurts and my throat's sore, so I'm not feeling so good.

(N1 は) N2 です。

(N1 wa) N2 desu.

(N1 is) N2.

田中：辞書はどこにありますか。

Tanaka: Jisho wa doko ni arimasu ka.

Where is the dictionary?

青木：机の上です。

Aoki: Tsukue no ue desu.

It's on the desk.

This pattern is the same as Basic Pattern 1 (*N1 wa N2 desu*), but here we show its use in conversation. The subject is often omitted since it is understood from context, and the predicate (which provides information about the subject) supplies the answer to a question in which an interrogative word has been used to ask for information concerning what, when, where, how, and so forth.

Formula

(N1 wa) N2 desu.

N1 = a noun acting as a subject; often omitted in conversation when understood from context

N2 = a noun providing information about the subject

Polite

関口：会社の工場はどこにありますか。

Sekiguchi: Kaisha no kōjō wa doko ni arimasu ka.

Where is the company factory located?

島田：千葉県です。

Shimada: Chiba-ken desu.

In Chiba prefecture.

小野：今日は何を食べましょうか。

Ono: Kyō wa nani o tabemashō ka.

What shall we eat today?

山下：そうですね。私はてんぷらですね。

Yamashita: Sō desu ne. Watashi wa tempura desu ne.
  (Watashi wa tempura o tabemasu.)

Well, I think I'll have tempura.

高橋：これからどこへ行きますか。

Takahashi: Kore kara doko e ikimasu ka.

Where are you going now?

岡田：日本橋です。

Okada: Nihonbashi desu. (Watashi wa Nihonbashi e iki-masu.)

To Nihonbashi.

Informal

BETWEEN MEN OR WOMEN

田中：辞書、どこにある？

Tanaka: Jisho, doko ni aru?

Where's the dictionary?

青木：机の上。

Aoki: Tsukue no ue. (Jisho wa tsukue no ue ni arimasu.)

On the desk.

Informal

BETWEEN WOMEN

洋子：お母さんはどこにいるの？

Yōko: Okāsan wa doko ni iru no?

Where's Mother?

聡子：隣の部屋よ。

Satoko: Tonari no heya yo. (Okasan wa tonari no heya ni imasu.)

In the next room.

恵：デパートで、何買いたいの？

Megumi: Depāto de, nani kaitai no?

What do you want to buy at the department store?

達子：長いスカートよ。

Tatsuko: Nagai sukāto yo. (Watashi wa nagai sukāto ga kaitai desu.)

A long skirt.

Basic Pattern 11 Adj Question with *dochira* and Answer with *hō*

1. **N1**と **N2**と どちらが**Adj** ですか。

   N1 to N2 to dochira ga Adj desu ka.

   Which one is Adj, N1 or N2?

   このケーキとそのケーキと、どちらが甘いですか。

   Kono kēki to sono kēki to dochira ga amai desu ka.

   Which is sweeter, this cake or that cake?

2. **N1** (**N2**) のほうが **Adj** です。

   N1 (N2) no hō ga Adj desu.

   N1 (N2) is Adj.

   そのケーキのほうが甘いです。

   Sono kēki no hō ga amai desu.

   That cake is sweeter.

This pattern shows how to ask "which" (*dochira*; or collo-quially, *dotchi*) of two things has more of a certain at-tribute (represented by an adjective), and then how to answer the question. The question usually begins with list-ing what the two things are, each followed by the particle *to* ("and" or "or"). Then the question is asked, using an interrogative word as the subject of the sentence. The question is answered by placing one's choice, followed by *no*, before the word *hō* ("side," "alternative"), which is the subject of the answer.

Formula 1

___

N1 to N2 to dochira ga Adj desu ka.

N1 = a noun representing the first choice being offered

N2 = a noun representing the second choice being offered

to = a particle following each of the nouns being com-pared

dochira = an interrogative word meaning "which"

Adj = an i-adjective or na-adjective providing informa-tion about the subject (the interrogative word)

Formula 2

___

N1(N2) no hō ga Adj desu.

N1 = a noun modifying the subject (*hō*)

N2 = a noun (representing an alternative choice) modi-fying the subject (*hō*)

hō = a noun acting as a subject ("side," "alternative")

Adj = an i-adjective or na-adjective providing informa-tion about the subject

江口：中国とインドと、どちらが人口が多い
んでしょうか。

Eguchi: Chūgoku to Indo to, dochira ga jinkō ga ōi 'n deshō ka.
Which country has the larger population, China or India.

岡本：中国のほうが多いでしょう。

Okamoto: Chūgoku no hō ga ōi deshō.
I think China's is larger.

BETWEEN WOMEN

片岡：てんぷらとお寿司とどっちが好き？

Kataoka: Tempura to osushi to dotchi ga suki?
Which do you prefer, tempura or sushi?

安部：お寿司。あなたは？

Abe: Osushi. Anata wa?
Sushi. How about you?

Variation **1** Adj Sentence Stating Preference with *hō* and *yori*

N1 のほう が N2 より Adj です。

N1 no hō ga N2 yori Adj desu.
N1 is more Adj than N2.

そのケーキのほうがこのケーキより甘いです。

Sono kēki no hō ga kono kēki yori amai desu.
That cake is sweeter than this.

This variation has almost the same meaning as the answer
in Basic Pattern 11 (*N1 no hō ga Adj desu*); the difference is

that this variation makes the object of comparison explicit by the use of *yori* ("more than"), which follows the noun that is the lesser of the two choices. In conversation, *N2 yori* is often omitted if it is understood from context, in which case Basic Pattern 11 and this variation end up being the same.

Formula

N1 no hō ga N2 yori Adj desu.

N1 = a noun modifying the subject (*hō*)

N2 = a noun that is an object of comparison

yori = a particle that follows the noun that is being compared to the subject; "more than"

Adj = an i-adjective or na-adjective giving information about the subject

Polite

小林：この山と富士山とどちらが高いんですか。

Kobayashi: Kono yama to Fujisan to dochira ga takai 'n desu ka.

Which is higher, this mountain or Mt. Fuji?

北川：富士山のほうがこの山より少し高いと思いますよ。

Kitagawa: Fujisan no hō ga kono yama yori sukoshi takai to omoimasu yo.

I think Mt. Fuji is a little bit higher than this mountain.

Informal

BETWEEN MEN

亀井：こっちのカメラとそっちと、どっちが得かなあ？

Kamei: Kotchi no kamera to sotchi to, dotchi ga toku ka naa?

Which is a better buy, this camera or that one?

植田：そっちのほうが、こっちよりいいんじゃない。

Ueda: Sotchi no hō ga kotchi yori ii 'n ja nai.

That one seems better than this one to me.

---

1. <u>N1</u> と <u>N2</u> と <u>N3</u> の中で、どれ が 一番 <u>Adj</u> ですか。

N1 to N2 to N3 no naka de, dore ga ichiban Adj desu ka.

Among N1, N2, and N3, which is the most Adj?

イチゴとミカンとリンゴの中で、どれが 一番好きですか。

Ichigo to mikan to ringo no naka de, dore ga ichiban suki desu ka.

Which do you like best, strawberries, oranges, or apples?

2. <u>N1</u> (<u>N2</u> / <u>N3</u>) が一番 <u>Adj</u> です。

N1 (N2 / N3) ga ichiban Adj desu.

N1 (N2 / N3) is most the Adj.

私はイチゴが一番好きです。

Watashi wa ichigo ga ichiban suki desu.

I like strawberries best.

This pattern shows how to ask which of three things is preferable or best in some way. The question is similar to Basic Pattern 11 (<u>N1 to N2 to dochira ga Adj desu ka</u>) in that the first two choices are each followed by *to* ("or") but different in that the third choice is followed by *no naka de* ("among"). Both the question and answer are distinguished by the fact that the adjective is preceded by *ichiban* ("most").

N1 to N2 to N3 no naka de, dore ga ichiban Adj desu ka.

N1 = a noun indicating the first of three choices

N2 = a noun indicating the second of three choices

N3 = a noun indicating the third of three choices

no naka de = "among"

ichiban = "most," indicating the superlative degree of the following adjective

Adj = an i-adjective or na-adjective providing information about the subject

N1 (N2 / N3) ga ichiban Adj desu.

N1 = a noun acting as the subject of the sentence

N2 = a noun indicating an alternative subject of the sentence

N3 = a noun indicating yet another alternative subject of the sentence

ichiban = "most," indicating the superlative degree of the following adjective

Adj = an i-adjective or na-adjective providing information about the subject

教授：大野さんと小泉さんと小沢さんの中で、誰が一番背が高いですか。

Kyōju: Ōno-san to Koizumi-san to Ozawa-san no naka de, dare ga ichiban se ga takai desu ka.

Professor: Who is the tallest, you (Ms. Ono), Ms. Koizumi, or Ms. Ozawa?

大野：小泉さんが一番高いです。

Ōno: Koizumi-san ga ichiban takai desu.

Ms. Koizumi is the tallest.

BETWEEN WOMEN

康子：一緒に映画に行きたいんだけど、火曜
日と水曜日と木曜日の中で、いつが一番都
合がいい？

*Yasuko: Issho ni eiga ni ikitai 'n da kedo, kayō-bi to suiyō-
bi to mokuyō-bi no naka de, itsu ga ichiban tsugō ga ii?*

I'd like to see a movie with you. Which day is most convenient—Tuesday, Wednesday, or Thursday?

一恵：そうね、水曜日が一番いいわ。

Kazue: Sō ne, suiyō-bi ga ichiban ii wa.

Well, Wednesday is best for me.

Basic Pattern **13** Adj Sentence Indicating Equality with *onaji kurai*

N1 は **N2** と 同じくらい (**Adj**) です。

N1 wa N2 to onaji kurai (Adj) desu.

N1 is about the same (Adj) as N2.

そのケーキはこのケーキと同じくらい甘い
です。

Sono kēki wa kono kēki to onaji kurai amai desu.

That cake is about as sweet as this one.

This pattern shows that two things are almost equal in some
attribute. The attribute is indicated by the adjective, which is
preceded by *onaji kurai* ("about the same"), but it may be
omitted from the sentence if it is understood from context.

<u>N1</u> wa <u>N2</u> to onaji kurai (<u>Adj</u>) desu.

N1 = a noun acting as the subject of the sentence

N2 = a noun that is being compared with the subject and is followed by *to*

onaji kurai = "about the same"

Adj = an i-adjective or na-adjective providing information about the subject, which may be omitted if understood from context

秋山：夏は東京とここと、どちらが蒸し暑いですか。

Akiyama: Natsu wa Tōkyō to koko to, dochira ga mushi-atsui desu ka.

Is summer more humid in Tokyo or here?

江口：東京はここと同じくらいじゃないですか。

Eguchi: Tōkyō wa koko to onaji kurai ja nai desu ka.

Tokyo must be about the same as here.

BETWEEN MEN

大西：この車と僕の車と、どっちが馬力が強い？

Ōnishi: Kono kuruma to boku no kuruma to, dotchi ga bariki ga tsuyoi?

Which has more power, this car or mine?

市川：ほとんど同じくらいだろう。

Ichikawa: Hotondo onaji kurai darō.

They must be about the same.

**N1 は N2 ほど I-adj くないです / Na-adj では
ありません。**

*N1 wa N2 hodo I-adj-ku nai desu / Na-adj dewa ari-
masen.*

N1 is not as much Adj as N2.

そのケーキはこのケーキほど甘くないです。

Sono kēki wa kono kēki hodo amaku nai desu.

That cake isn't as sweet as this one.

Whereas Basic Pattern 13 (*N1 wa N2 to onaji kurai (Adj) desu*)
expressed the idea that two things were basically the same, this
pattern indicates that one thing does not have a certain
attribute to the extent that another thing does. The subject is
the thing that comes out unfavorably in the comparison; that
which is compared favorably is followed by *hodo*, which
indicates extent and could be translated as "to the extent of"
or "as much as." The adjective appears in its negative form.

Formula

**N1 *wa* N2 *hodo* I-adj-*ku nai desu* / Na-adj *dewa ari-
masen.***

N1 = a noun acting as a subject

N2 = a noun being compared to the subject

hodo = a particle following the noun being compared;
  "to the extent of"

I-adj = an i-adjective in the negative form (*-ku nai*) providing information about the subject

Na-adj = a na-adjective in the negative form (followed
  by *dewa arimasen*) providing information about the
  subject

高木：山本さんはこの頃海外出張が多いですね。

Takagi: Yamamoto-san wa konogoro kaigai-shutchō ga ōi desu ne.

Mr. Yamamoto, you often go on overseas business trips these days, don't you.

山本：ええ、でも高木さんほど多くないですよ。

Yamamoto: Ee, demo Takagi-san hodo ōku nai desu yo.

Yes, but not as often as you do.

BETWEEN WOMEN

早苗：この辺静かね。

Sanae: Kono hen shizuka ne.

It is quiet around here, isn't it.

さおり：でもお宅ほど静かじゃないわ。

Saori: Demo otaku hodo shizuka ja nai wa.

Yes, but it isn't as quiet as your place.

Basic Patterns 15-17

CHAPTER 4

This chapter introduces patterns in the subjunctive mood ("if") and hearsay (secondhand information) for adjectives and nouns, with a number of variations on each basic pattern. Basic Pattern 15 and its three variations all deal with different ways of saying "if," both in hypothetical situations ("If I were president …") and in conditional ones ("On the condition that you pass the test …"). In many cases, these patterns are interchangable with little difference in meaning, but even then each pattern retains a core meaning that is different from the others. We will try to point out a few of these differences in core meaning.

Basic Pattern ⟨15⟩ **Subjunctive Adj Sentence with *tara/dattara***

N は / が Adj1 たら / だったら Adj2 です。
N wa / ga Adj1 -tara / dattara Adj2 desu.
If N is Adj1, then Adj2.

あの車が小さかったら便利りです。

Ano kuruma ga chiisakattara benri desu.

If that car is small, it will be convenient.

田中さんが元気だったらうれしいです。

Tanaka-san ga genki dattara ureshii desu.

I'll be happy if Ms. Tanaka is well. (i.e., I hope Ms. Tanaka is well.

This pattern shows the subjunctive mood with a *-tara* ending for i-adjectives and *dattara* following na-adjectives. While both of these mean "if," the core meaning is "supposing that" or "if … should happen."

For information about subjunctive verb patterns, see Basic Pattern 47.

Formula

<u>N</u> wa / ga <u>Adj1</u> -tara / dattara <u>Adj2</u> desu.

N = a noun acting as a subject

Adj1 = an i-adjective or na-adjective in the subjunctive form

-tara = the subjunctive form of an i-adjective: "if"

dattara = the subjective form of *da*, which follows a na-adjective: "if"

Adj2 = an i-adjective or na-adjective providing information about the subject

Polite

明日天気が良かったら、嬉しいです。

Ashita tenki ga yokattara, ureshii desu.

If it's fine tommorow, I'll be happy. (i.e., I hope it's fine tomorrow.)

料理が辛かったら、あまり食べられません。

Ryōri ga karakattara, amari taberaremasen.

If the food is spicy, I can't eat much.

BETWEEN WOMEN

黒田：世界中が平和だったらいいわね。

Kuroda: Sekai-jū ga heiwa dattara ii wa ne.

It would be wonderful if the whole world were at peace.

岡本：そうね。でも無理ね。

Okamoto; Sō ne. Demo muri ne.

You're right. But it's impossible.

Variation 1 · Subjunctive Adj Sentence with *to/da to*

<u>N</u> は / が <u>Adj1</u> と / だと <u>Adj2</u> です。

N wa / ga Adj1 to / da to Adj2 desu.

It is Adj2 if N is Adj1.

天気がいいとうれしいです。

Tenki ga ii to ureshii desu.

I'm glad when the weather is good.

田中さんは元気だとうるさいです。

Tanaka-san wa genki da to urusai desu.

When Mr. Tanaka gets energetic, he's a real bother.

While this variation indicates the subjunctive mood ("if"), both hypothetical and conditional, the nuance is that if (or when) one thing happens, then something else will happen *without fail.* In translation, *to* seems to vary between "if" and "when." While Basic Pattern 15 and Variations 2 and 3 can end with a command (i.e., "If this happens, do that"), this variation cannot. Further, with *to*, the condition to be fulfilled has often already being fulfilled, as in the second sample sentence below under "Informal (Between Mother and Daughter)," where it is already late.

N wa / ga <u>Adj1</u> to / da to <u>Adj2</u> desu.

N = a noun acting as the subject of the sentence or (when followed by *ga*) the subject of Adj1

Adj1 = an i-adjective or na-adjective in the subjunctive (presenting a condition)

to = a particle indicating a conditional situation

Adj2 = an i-adjective or na-adjective providing information about the subject

店が遠いと不便です。

Mise ga tōi to fuben desu.

It's inconvenient when the shops are far away.

雨が多いと緑がきれいです。

Ame ga ōi to midori ga kirei desu.

The greenery looks lovely when it rains a lot.

BETWEEN MOTHER AND DAUGHTER

娘：知子に電話しよう。

Musume: Tomoko ni denwa shiyō.

I think I'll call Tomoko.

母：あまり遅いと、ご迷惑よ。

Haha: Amari osoi to, gomeiwaku yo.

It'll be a bother if you call her so late. (If you call this late, you'll make a nuisance of yourself.)

Variation 2 Subjunctive Adj Sentence with *kereba*

<u>N</u> は / が <u>*I-adj*</u>ければ <u>Adj</u> です。

N wa / ga I-adj-kereba Adj desu.

It is Adj if N is Adj.

このスープは温かければ、おいしいです。

Kono sūpu wa atatakakereba, oishii desu.

If this soup were hot, it would be quite good.

参加者が多ければ、にぎやかです。

Sanka-sha ga ōkereba, nigiyaka desu.

If many people take part, it will be very lively.

While this variation indicates the subjunctive mood ("if"), both hypothetical and conditional, its main emphasis resides in the conditional ("providing that …," "on the condition that"). When a na-adjective is used in this pattern, it must be followed by *nara*. The final adjective in this sentence (the predicate) may be replaced by a verb.

Formula

<u>*N*</u> *wa / ga* <u>*I-adj*</u>*-kereba* <u>*Adj*</u> *desu.*

N = a noun acting as the subject of an I-adj (when followed by *ga*) or the sentence as a whole

I-adj = an i-adjective in the subjunctive

kereba = the subjunctive form of an i-adjective

Adj = an i-adjective or na-adjective providing information about the subject of the sentence

In the subjunctive, the sentence often ends in such words as *deshō*, *darō*, *datta deshō*, *dattarō*, etc., which emphasize feelings of expectation, conjecture, hope, wish, or regret, depending on whether or not the condition is fulfilled.

Polite

政治家がもっと頭が良ければ、国家は安全だっただろう。

Seiji-ka ga motto atama ga yokereba, kokka wa anzen datta darō.

If politicians were smarter, the nation would have been secure.

立花さんの仕事がこんなに忙しくなければ、健康だったでしょう。

Tachibana-san no shigoto ga konna ni isogashiku nakereba, kenkō datta deshō.

If Mr. Tachibana hadn't been so busy with his work, he would have been healthy.

Informal

BETWEEN MALE STUDENTS

高木：このフランス語の文、わかる？

Takagi: Kono Furansu-go no bun, wakaru?

Do you understand this French sentence?

島田：もっとやさしかったら、僕でもわかる
　　　と思うけど、こんなに難しければ、無理だ。

*Shimada: Motto yasashikattara, boku demo wakaru to
omou kedo, konna ni muzukashikereba muri da.*

If it were a little easier, I think that even I could understand
it, but it's out of the question with something this hard.

Informal

BETWEEN WOMEN

進藤：こんなに大勢の若い人たちが死んだの？

Shindō: Konna ni ōzei no wakai hitotachi ga shinda no?

Did that many young people die?

関口：そうよ、戦争がなければ、この人達は
　　　長生きできたのに。

*Sekiguchi: Sō yo, sensō ga nakereba, kono hitotachi wa
nagaiki dekita no ni.*

Yes, they did. If there hadn't been a war, they could have
lived long lives.

Variation **3** **Subjunctive Adj Sentence with *nara***

<u>N1</u> は / が <u>Adj1</u> / <u>N2</u> なら <u>Adj2</u> です。

N1 wa / ga Adj1 / N2 nara Adj2 desu.

It is Adj2 if N1 is / Adj1 / N2.

母が丈夫ならうれしいです。

Haha ga jōbu nara ureshii desu.

If my mother is in good health, then I'm happy.

この仕事は関口さんなら簡単です。

Kono shigoto wa Sekiguchi-san nara kantan desu.

If left to Sekiguchi, this job's a snap.

In this pattern, *nara* (meaning "if") can follow nouns, adjectives, and verbs. Just as with other patterns dealing with the subjunctive above, this pattern deals with hypothetical and conditional situations. Somewhat different from the others, however, *nara* is often restrictive in the conditions it points to, and could be translated as "only if." Also, when referring to conditions, the speaker may have reason to believe that the condition has already been fulfilled (as in both the examples under "Polite" below, where the speaker has some reason to believe that "the news of the accident isn't true" and that the form is written in a complicated style). The sample sentences in this section deal only with na-adjectives and nouns before *nara*, but i-adjectives and verbs can also appear in that position. I-adjectives, however, appear rather infrequently before *nara*, and their use has not been exemplified here.

Formula

N1 wa / ga Adj1 / N2 nara Adj2 desu.

N1 = a noun acting as the subject of the sentence or (when followed by *ga*) of Adj1

Adj1 = an i-adjective or na-adjective that states a condition

N2 = a noun that states a condition

nara = a particle ("if") indicating a condition or hypothesis

Adj2 = an i-adjective or na-adjective providing information about the subject

---

Polite

その事故のニュースが間違いなら嬉しいのですが。

Sono jiko no nyūsu ga machigai nara ureshii no desu ga.
I'll be very happy if the news of the accident isn't true.

この文章が英語なら、もっとやさしいです。

Kono bunshō ga Eigo nara, motto yasashii desu.

If this sentence / passage were in English, it would be much simpler.

Informal

BETWEEN MAN AND WOMAN

孝夫：子供たちが静かなら、さびしいよ。

Takao: Kodomo-tachi ga shizuka nara, sabishii yo.

If the children are quiet, I feel lonely.

加奈子：そうね。でも、うるさければ大変でしょう。

Kanako: Sō ne. Demo, urusakereba taihen deshō.

That's true. But if they're noisy, that isn't so great either.

Basic Pattern 16 Adj Sentence about Appearance with -sō

N は Adj そうです。

N wa Adj-sō desu.

N looks like Adj.

外は寒そうです。

Soto wa samusō desu.

It looks cold outside.

課長は今忙しそうです。

Kachō wa ima isogashisō desu.

The section manager looks busy now.

This pattern indicates how something appears to the speaker. What is being referred to must be the result of the speaker's direct observation or experience, not something heard from another party. It is formed by placing the suffix *sō* (which refers to outward appearance) after an i-adjective from which the final "i" has been dropped or directly after a na-adjective. See also Basic Pattern 47 for *sō* with verbs.

Formula

N wa Adj-sō desu.
N = a noun acting as a subject

Adj = an i-adjective (with the final *i* dropped) or a na-adjective)

sō = a suffix referring to outward appearance that is appended to i-adjectives from which the final "i" has been dropped and directly to na-adjectives

Polite

この料理はおいしそうです。
Kono ryōri wa oishisō desu.
This food looks good.

経済の問題は複雑で、解決は難しそうです。
Keizai no mondai wa fukuzatsu de, kaiketsu wa muzukashisō desu.
The economic problems are complicated and appear difficult to solve.

Informal

BETWEEN WOMEN

菊江：どの映画見に行く？
Kikue: Dono eiga mi ni iku?
Which movie shall we go to see?

夏子：そうね。このフランス映画、どうかし
　　　ら？　面白そうよ。

Natsuko: Sō ne. Kono Furansu eiga dō kashira? Omoshi-rosō yo.

Well, how about this French movie? It looks interesting.

大竹：田舎のご両親、お元気だった？

Ōtake: Inaka no goryōshin, ogenki datta?

Were your parents back home well?

小野：ありがとう。元気そうだったわ。

Ono: Arigatō. Genki-sō datta wa.

Thank you. They looked fine.

Variation ① **Negative Adj Sentence about Appearance with -sō**

<u>N</u> は <u>Adj</u> そうではありません。

N wa Adj-sō dewa arimasen.

N doesn't look like Adj.

この料理はおいしそうではありません。

Kono ryōri wa oishisō dewa arimasen.

This food doesn't look good.

あの二人は幸せそうではありません。

Ano futari wa shiawase-sō dewa arimasen.

Those two don't look happy.

This variation shows the negative form of Basic Pattern 16 (<u>N</u> wa <u>Adj</u>-sō desu). Instead of *dewa arimasen*, *ja arimasen* can be used. The latter is used in speech while the former appears in polite conversation and writing.

N wa Adj-sō dewa arimasen.

N = a noun acting as a subject

Adj = an i-adjective (with the final *i* dropped and *sō* appended) or a na-adjective followed by *sō*

Polite

この本は面白そうではありません。

Kono hon wa omoshirosō dewa arimasen.

This book doesn't look interesting.

この子はまだ眠そうではありません。

Kono ko wa mada nemusō dewa arimasen.

The baby doesn't seem to be sleepy yet.

Informal

BETWEEN WOMEN IN A PARK

酒井：みんな楽しそうに遊んでいるわね。

Sakai: Minna tanoshisō ni asonde iru wa ne.

They all seem to be playing so happily.

井上：そうね。でもどうして家の子だけ楽し そうじゃないのかしら

Inoue: Sō ne. Demo dōshite uchi no ko dake tanoshisō ja nai no kashira.

That's right. But why is it that only my child doesn't seem to be having fun?

Informal

BETWEEN COLLEGE GIRLS

ゆり子：昨日試験勉強した？

Yuriko: Kinō shiken benkyō shita?

Did you study for the exam yesterday?

敦子：それが全然できなかったの。

Atsuko: Sorega zenzen dekinakatta no.

As a matter of fact, I didn't do anything at all.

ゆり子：でもちっとも心配そうじゃないのね。

Yuriko: Demo chitto mo shinpai-sō ja nai no ne.

But you don't look worried at all.

<u>N</u> は <u>Adj</u> そう / だそうです。

N wa Adj sō / da sō desu.

They say N is Adj.

北海道の冬は寒いそうです。

Hokkaidō no fuyu wa samui sō desu

They say winter in Hokkaido is cold.

沖縄の海はきれいだそうです。

Okinawa no umi wa kirei da sō desu.

They say the sea around Okinawa is beautiful.

This pattern is a means of passing on information learned from another party. It is objective in tone and can follow either present or past forms. What follows *sō* (either *da* or *desu*), however, must be in the present tense. If you want to give the source of the information, add *N ni yoru to* ("According to N") at the beginning of the sentence.

Formula

<u>N</u> wa <u>Adj</u> *sō* / *da sō desu.*

N = a noun acting as a subject

Adj = an i-adjective followed by *sō* or an na-adjective followed by *da sō*

ハワイのパイナップルは甘くて、おいしいそうです。

Hawai no painappuru wa amakute, oishii sō desu.

I hear that Hawaiian pineapples are sweet and tasty.

宇宙から見ると、地球は青くてきれいだそうです。

Uchū kara miru to, chikyū wa aokute kirei da sō desu.

They say the earth is blue and beautiful when seen from space.

BETWEEN MEN

河合：弟さんの新しい車、調子はどう？

Kawai: Otōto-san no atarashii kuruma, chōshi wa dō?

How's your kid brother's new car running?

渋川：なかなかいいそうだよ。

Shibukawa: Nakanaka ii sō da yo.

I hear that it couldn't be better.

部長：東京商事の今年の業績について、何か聞いてる？

Buchō: Tokyo Shōji no kotoshi no gyōseki ni tsuite, nanika kiite 'ru?

Did you hear anything about Tokyo Trading's business results this year?

課長：それが、今年はだめだそうですよ。

Kachō: Sorega, kotoshi wa dame da sō desu yo.

As it happens, I hear that this year is not good.

1. <u>N</u> は **I-adj** くないそうです。

N wa I-adj-ku nai sō desu.

They say N isn't Adj.

今年の冬はあまり寒くないそうです。

Kotoshi no fuyu wa amari samuku nai sō desu.

They say this winter won't be very cold.

2. <u>N</u> は **Na-adj** ではないそうです。

N wa Na-adj dewa nai sō desu.

They say N isn't Adj.

課長によると、このデータは正確ではないそうです。

Kachō ni yoru to, kono dēta wa seikaku dewa nai sō desu.

According to the section manager, this data is not accurate.

This pattern is the negative version of Basic Pattern 17 (<u>*N wa Adj [da] sō desu*</u>). Instead of *dewa nai*, *ja nai* can be used for slightly more emphasis and a more colloquial tone. To refer to something that occurred in the past, *I-adj-ku nai* is replaced by *I-adj-ku nakatta*, and *Na-adj dewa nai* is replaced by *Na-adj dewa nakatta*. For an example of the former, see the dialogue under "Informal, Between Women" below.

Formula 1

<u>*N wa I-adj-ku nai sō desu.*</u>

N = a noun acting as a subject

I-adj = the negative form of an i-adjective in the present or past tense *sō* = a suffix referring to hearsay that directly follows the negative forms of i-adjectives and na-adjectives

Polite

新しいパソコンは、そんなに高くないそうです。

Atarashii pasokon wa sonna ni takaku nai sō desu.
They say that the new PCs aren't so expensive.

この機械の効率は良くないそうです。

Kono kikai no kōritsu wa yoku nai sō desu.
They say that this machine is not very efficient.

Informal

BETWEEN MEN

小出：谷商事の新製品の評判はどう？

Koide: Tani Shōji no shin-seihin no hyōban wa dō?
What's the reputation of Tani Trading's new products?

大山：それが、あまり良くないそうだよ。

Ōyama: Sorega, amari yoku nai sō da yo.
As it happens, I hear it's not very good.

Informal

BETWEEN WOMEN

小林：新しい店のケーキ、おいしいのかしら。

Kobayashi: Atarashii mise no kēki, oishii no kashira.
I wonder if the cake at the new shop is any good.

片岡：黒田さんが言ってたけど、そんなにおいしくなかったそうよ。

Kataoka: Kuroda-san ga itte 'ta kedo, sonna ni oishiku nakatta sō yo.

Ms. Kuroda was talking about that, and I understand it wasn't that good.

_N_ wa _Na-Adj_ dewa nai sō desu.

N = a noun acting as a subject

Na-adj = a na-adjective providing information about
the subject

奥野先生はあまりお丈夫じゃないそうです。

Okuno sensei wa amari ojōbu ja nai sō desu.

They say that our teacher, Mr. Okuno, isn't very strong.

ニューヨークの地下鉄は最近では危険ではないそうです。

_Nyūyōku no chikatetsu wa saikin de wa kiken dewa nai sō
desu._

I hear that New York subways are not dangerous these days.

BETWEEN WOMEN

笠原：この歌きれいね。初めて聴いたわ。

Kasahara: Kono uta kirei ne. Hajimete kiita wa.

This song is beautiful. It's my first time to hear it.

栗原：そうなの？　アメリカでは今とても有名だけど、日本ではまだ有名じゃないそうね。

_Kurihara: Sō na no? Amerika de wa ima totemo yūmei da
kedo, Nihon de wa mada yūmei ja nai sō ne._

Is that right? It's very well known in America now, but I
understand that in Japan it's not well known yet.

斉藤：林さん、明日手術だから心配でしょうね。

Saitō: Hayashi-san, ashita shujutsu da kara shinpai deshō ne.

Mr. Hayashi is having an operation tomorrow. He must
be worried about it.

小池：それが、ちっとも心配じゃないそうよ。

Koike: Sorega, chittomo shinpai ja nai sō yo.

You would think so, but I hear that he's not worried at all.

<u>N1</u> は <u>N2</u> / <u>Adj</u> だろうと思います。

N1 wa N2 / Adj darō to omoimasu.

I think N1 is N2 / Adj.

アラスカの冬は寒いだろうと思います。

Arasuka no fuyu wa samui darō to omoimasu.

In winter it must be cold in Alaska.

This pattern offers a means of presenting what one supposes or conjectures with some confidence but not with absolute certainty. This is conveyed by *darō*, which means "likely" or "probably," and *omoimasu*, "to think, suppose." Since this pattern ends in a verb, strictly speaking it belongs in Part 2 (Verb Sentences), but we have chosen to interpret it as an adjective sentence followed by the fixed and suffix-like *darō to omoimasu*. It differs from Basic Patterns 16 and 17 in that the information it conveys need not be based entirely on appearance or hearsay.

Formula

<u>N1</u> wa <u>N2</u> / <u>Adj</u> darō to omoimasu.

N1 = a noun acting as a subject

N2 = a noun providing information about the subject

Adj = an i-adjective or na-adjective providing information about the subject

darō = "probably," "likely"

to omoimasu = polite form of *to omou*; "to think, suppose"

この道は夜暗いだろうと思います。

Kono michi wa yoru kurai darō to omoimasu.

This street must be dark at night.

今頃海は穏やかだろうと思います。

Imagoro umi wa odayaka darō to omoimasu.

The sea must be calm about now.

あの方は、フランス人だろうと思います。

Ano kata wa, Furansu-jin darō to omoimasu.

I think he is French. / He must be French.

BETWEEN MEN

大野：菊池君の家、駅から近いの？

Ōno: Kikuchi-kun no uchi, eki kara chikai no?

Is Kikuchi's house near the station?

佐々木：いや、駅まで車で来るそうだから、
遠いんだろうと思うよ。

Sasaki: Iya, eki made kuruma de kuru sō da kara, tōi 'n darō to omou yo.

No, I hear he goes to the station by car, so it must be a good distance.

ON THE FREEWAY

伊藤：5時までに、飛行場に着けるかな？

Itō: Goji made ni, hikō-jō ni tsukeru ka na?

Can we make it to the airport by five?

小沢：道がすいてるから、大丈夫だろうと思うよ。

Ozawa: Michi ga suite 'ru kara, daijōbu darō to omou yo.

I think we can make it since traffic is light.

内山：小池まだ来ない？

Uchiyama: Koike mada konai?

Koike hasn't shown up yet?

小泉：うん、また電車の事故だろうと思うよ。

Koizumi: Un, mata densha no jiko darō to omou yo.

No, there must have been another train accident.

Verb Sentences

This part of the dictionary introduces thirty-three patterns based on the third most fundamental type of Japanese sentence: the verb sentence. A verb sentence is one in which a verb comes at the end of the sentence and acts as the predicate (i.e., provides information about the subject).

Basic Pattern 18

In this chapter, we will see that there are two verbs that convey the information that something exists, both of which in English would be expressed by "to be." The first one, *arimasu*, is basically used for objects that are not capable of movement under their own power; the second, *imasu*, is basically used for objects that are capable of such movement.

Basic Pattern 18 ▸ Verbs of Existence for Inanimate/Animate Objects

1. **N**がV(**あります**)。
   N ga V (arimasu).
   N exists.

   ピアノがあります。
   Piano ga arimasu.
   There is a piano.

2. **N**がV(**います**)。
   N ga V (imasu).
   N exists.

> **子供がいます。**
> *Kodomo ga imasu.*
> There is a child.

This basic pattern indicates existence of both animate and inanimate objects. If the verb *arimasu* is used, the noun should be something that we do not ordinarily think of as being capable of self-movement. And if you use the verb *imasu*, the noun should be something that moves under its own power, such as human beings, animals, or insects.

Formula 1

<u>N</u> ga V (arimasu).
N exists.
N = a noun (inaminate object) acting as a subject
V = a verb (*arimasu*) showing existence

Polite

テレビがあります。
Terebi ga arimasu.
There is a TV.

電話があります。
Denwa ga arimasu.
There is a telephone.

Informal

BETWEEN WOMEN

佐藤：今晩、面白い番組あるわよ。
Satō: Konban, omoshiroi bangumi aru wa yo.
There is an interesting program tonight.

笠井：本当？
Kasai: Hontō?
Really?

_N_ ga V (imasu).
N exists.
N = a noun (animate object) acting as a subject
V = a verb (*imasu*) showing existence

小さい犬がいます。
Chiisai inu ga imasu.
There is a small dog.

女の子がいます。
Onna no ko ga imasu.
There is a girl.

女の子：猫がいるわ。
Onna no ko: Neko ga iru wa.
Girl: There's a cat.

You will have noticed that in the informal examples given above the verb changed from the *-masu* form to the plain form (*aru* and *iru*). In casual speech, the plain form is often used and the particle (*wa* or *ga*) following the noun is dropped, as examples given below will demonstrate. For more information about changes in verb form, please refer to my *Japanese Verbs at a Glance*.

This pattern sometimes indicates possession ("have"), as the following examples show.

金井さんは車があります。

Kanai-san wa kuruma ga arimasu.
Mr. Kanai has a car.

横田さんはお子さんがいます。

Yokota-san wa okosan ga imasu.
Ms. Yokota has a child.

Variation 1 — Verbs of Existence with *mo* after the Subject

1. <u>N</u>もV（あります）。
N mo V (arimasu).
N also exists.

パソコンもあります。

Pasokon mo arimasu.
There is also a computer. / I have a computer also.

2. <u>N</u>もV（います）。
N mo V (imasu).
N also exists.

男の子もいます。

Otoko no ko mo imasu.
There is also a boy. / I have a son also.

In this variation of Basic Pattern 18 (<u>N</u> *ga V [arimasu/ imasu]*), *mo* ("also") replaces *ga*, indicating "There is also N." If needed, *mo* may be repeated two or three times, as in *N1 mo N2 mo arimasu* ("There is also N1 and N2").

<u>N</u> mo V (arimasu).

N also exists.

N = a noun (inanimate object) acting as a subject

V = a verb (*arimasu*) showing existence

mo = a particle meaning "also"

ラジオもあります。

Rajio mo arimasu.

There is also a radio. / I have a radio also.

車もあります。

Kuruma mo arimasu.

There is also a car. / I have a car also.

BETWEEN WOMEN

佐藤：夜音楽番組あるわよ。

Satō: Yoru ongaku-bangumi aru wa yo.

There is a music program at night.

笠井：朝もあるわよ。

Kasai: Asa mo aru wa yo.

There's also one in the morning.

<u>N</u> mo V (imasu).

N also exists.

N = a noun (animate object) acting as a subject

V = a verb (*imasu*) showing existence

mo = a particle meaning "also"

青い魚もいます。

Aoi sakana mo imasu.

There is also a blue fish.

フランス人の女の人もいます。

Furansu-jin no onna no hito mo imasu.

There is also a French woman.

男の子：赤い魚がいるよ。

Otoko no ko: Akai sakana ga iru yo.

Boy: There is a red fish.

女の子：青い魚もいるわ。

Onna no ko: Aoi sakana mo iru wa.

Girl: There is also a blue fish.

Variation 2 — Verbs of Existence in Questions

1. **N** が V (あります)か。

   N ga V (arimasu) ka.

   Does N exist?

   ## 細かいお金がありますか。

   Komakai okane ga arimasu ka.

   Do you have any change?

2. **N** が V (います)か。

   N ga V (imasu) ka.

   Does N exist?

   ## 山本さんがいますか。

   Yamamoto-san ga imasu ka.

   Is Mr. Yamamoto in / there?

In this variation of Basic Pattern 18 (*N ga V [arimasu/imasu]*), a statement is transformed into a question by adding *ka* to the end of the sentence. Variation 1 of Basic Pattern 18 (*N mo arimasu/imasu*) can also be transformed into a question in the same way.

Formula 1

N ga V (arimasu) ka.

Does N exist?

N = a noun (inanimate object) or interrogative word acting as a subject

V = a verb (*arimasu*) showing existence

ka = a particle indicating a question when placed at the end of a sentence

Polite

久保：茶碗がありますか。

Kubo: Chawan ga arimasu ka.

Are there any teabowls?

井上：はい、茶碗が三つあります。

Inoue: Hai, chawan ga mittsu arimasu.

Yes, there are three teabowls.

Informal

久保：茶碗ある？

Kubo: Chawan aru?

Are there any teabowls?

井上：うん、茶碗が三つあるよ。

Inoue: Un, chawan ga mittsu aru yo.

Yes, there are three.

_N_ _ga_ V _(imasu) ka._

Does N exist?

N = a noun (animate object) or interrogative word acting as a subject

V = a verb (_imasu_) showing existence

_ka_ = a particle indicating a question when placed at the
end of a sentence

Polite

岩佐：誰がいますか。

Iwasa: Dare ga imasu ka.

Who's there?

川瀬：課長も部長もいますよ。

Kawase: Kachō mo buchō mo imasu yo.

Both the section manager and department director.

Informal

岩佐：誰がいる？

Iwasa: Dare ga iru?

Who is there?

川瀬：課長も部長もいる。

Kawase: Kachō mo buchō mo iru.

Both the section manager and department director.

Variation **3** Verbs of Existence with Interrogatives

1. _Interrog_ か V (あります)か。

Interrog ka V (arimasu) ka.

Does any Interrog exist?

何かありますか。

Nani ka arimasu ka.

Is there anything?

2. **_Interrog_ か V (います)か。**

   Interrog ka V (imasu) ka.

   Dose any Interrog exist?

   誰かいますか。

   Dare ka imasu ka.

   Is anyone there?

This variation of Basic Pattern 18 (_N ga V [arimasu/ imasu]_) is similar to Variation 2. Here, however, the pronoun acting as the subject of the sentence (an interrogative word) is followed by *ka* instead of *ga*. Whether the interrogative is followed by *ka* or *ga* is of utmost importance. For example, compare: *Dare ga imasu ka?* ("Who's there?") and *Dare ka imasu ka* ("Is anyone there?").

◖Formula 1◗

Interrog ka V (arimasu) ka.

Does any Interrog exist?

Interrog = an interrogative word indicating an inanimate object

ka = a particle indicating uncertainty concerning the word that precedes it

V = a verb (*arimasu*) showing existence

ka = a particle indicating a question when placed at the end of a sentence

久保：何かありますか。

Kubo: Nani ka arimasu ka.

Is there anything? / Do you have anything?

**井上：はい、あります。牛乳と肉と野菜があ
ります。**

Inoue: Hai, arimasu. Gyūnyū to niku to yasai ga arimasu.

Yes, there is (I do). There's milk, meat, and vegetables.

久保：何かある？

Kubo: Nani ka aru?

Is there anything? / Do you have anything?

井上：うん、牛乳と肉と野菜があるよ。

Inoue: Un, gyūnyū to niku to yasai ga aru yo.

Yeah, there's milk, meat, and veggies.

Interrog ka V (imasu) ka.

Does any Interrog exist?

Interrog = an interrogative word indicating an animate object

ka = a particle indicating uncertainty concerning the word that precedes it

V = a verb (*imasu*) showing existence

ka = a particle indicating a question when placed at the end of a sentence

岩佐：誰かいますか。

Iwasa: Dare ka imasu ka.

Is anyone there?

川瀬：女の人がいますよ。

Kawase: Onna no hito ga imasu yo.

There's a woman.

Informal

BETWEEN MEN

岩佐：誰かいる？

Iwasa: Dare ka iru?

Is anyone there?

川瀬：女の人がいるよ。

Kawase: Onna no hito ga iru yo.

There's a woman.

Variation **4** Verbs of Existence in the Negative

1. N が / は V（ありません）。

N ga / wa V (arimasen).

N does not exist.

牛乳はありません。

Gyūnyū wa arimasen.

There isn't any milk.

2. N が / は V（いません）。

N ga / wa V (imasen).

N does not exist.

子供がいません。

Kodomo ga imasen.

There aren't any children. / I have no children.

This variation is a negative statement based on Basic Pattern 18 (_N ga V [arimasu/imasu]_). The particles _wa_ and _ga_ are used interchangeably according to context. (About particle usage, see my _All about Particles_.)

Formula 1

**N ga / wa V (arimasen).**
N does not exist.
N = a noun (inanimate object) acting as a subject
V = a verb (_arimasu_) showing existence

Polite

英語の辞書がありません。
Eigo no jisho ga arimasen.
There aren't any English dictionaries.

Informal

BETWEEN WOMEN

美加：英語の辞書ある？
Mika: Eigo no jisho aru?
Is there an English dictionary? / Do you have an English dictionary?

祐子：ないのよ。
Yūko: Nai no yo.
No, there isn't. / No, I don't.

Formula 2

**N ga / wa V (imasen).**
N does not exist.
N = a noun (animate object) acting as a subject
V = a verb (_imasu_) showing existence

先生は教室にいません。
Sensei wa kyōshitsu ni imasen.
The teacher isn't in the classroom.

Informal

BETWEEN MALE STUDENTS

洋：先生いる？
Hiroshi: Sensei iru?
Is the teacher in?

孝：いないよ。
Takashi: Inai yo.
No, he isn't.

Variation **5** Negative Verbs of Existence with *mo* after the Subject

1. <u>N</u>も V（ありません）。
N mo V (arimasen).
There isn't any N.

何もありません。
Nani mo arimasen.
There isn't anything.

2. <u>N</u>も V（いません）。
N mo V (imasen).
There isn't any N.

誰もいません。
Dare mo imasen.
There isn't anyone.

In this variation on Basic Pattern 18 (*N ga V [arimasu/ imasu]*), there are two important points: 1) the noun that is the subject of the sentence is a word such as *dare* ("who"), *itsu* ("when"), or *doko* ("where"); 2) the particle *mo* in this pattern does not mean "also," but rather "none of" or "any."

Formula 1

<u>N</u> *mo V (arimasen).*
There isn't any N.

N = a noun (i.e., a word such as *nani* ["what"]) indicating something inanimate and acting as the subject of the sentence

V = a verb (*arimasu*) showing existence

Polite

原：今面白い番組がありますか。
Hara: Ima omoshiroi bangumi ga arimasu ka.
Are there any interesting programs now?
野田：何もありません。
Noda: Nani mo arimasen.
There's nothing at all.

Informal

BETWEEN WOMEN

洋子：今面白い番組ある？
Yōko: Ima omoshiroi bangumi aru?
Are there any interesting programs now?
幸子：何もないわ。
Sachiko: Nani mo nai wa.
There aren't any at all.

N mo V (imasen).

There isn't any N.

N = a noun (i.e., a word such as *dare* ["who"]) indicating something animate and acting as the subject of the sentence

V = a verb (*imasu*) showing existence

Polite

今誰もいません。

Ima dare mo imasen.

There isn't anyone now.

何もいません。

Nani mo imasen.

There aren't any (living things) at all. / There aren't any animals.

Note in the last example sentence that *nani* can refer to animals when combined with *imasu*.

Informal

MAN

今誰もいないよ。

Ima dare mo inai yo.

There isn't anyone (here or there) now.

Informal

WOMAN

何もいないわ。

Nani mo inai wa.

There aren't any (living things) at all. / There aren't any animals.

1a. N が V (ありました)。

N ga V (arimashita).

N existed.

事故がありました。

Jiko ga arimashita.

There was an accident.

1b. N が V (いました)。

N ga V (imashita).

N existed.

黒い鳥がいました。

Kuroi tori ga imashita.

There was a black bird.

2a. N が V (ありませんでした)。

N ga V (arimasen deshita).

N did not exist.

タクシーがありませんでした。

Takushī ga arimasen deshita.

There were no taxis.

2b. N が V (いませんでした)。

N ga V (imasen deshita).

N did not exist.

日本人がいませんでした。

Nihon-jin ga imasen deshita.

There were no Japanese.

This variation on Pattern 18 (<u>N</u> *ga V [arimasu/imasu]*) consists of the past positive tenses (1a-b) and the past negative tenses (2a-b) of *arimasu* and *imasu*. The past positive tense is formed by changing the *masu* ending into *mashita*, and the past negative tense by changing *masu* into *masen deshita*.

Formula 1a

Past Tense of *arimasu*

<u>N</u> *ga V (arimashita).*
N existed.

N = a noun (inanimate object) acting as the subject of the sentence

V = a verb (*arimashita*) in the past tense showing existence

Polite

高橋：冷たい飲み物がありましたか。
Takahashi: Tsumetai nomimono ga arimashita ka.
Were there any cold drinks?

吉田：オレンジ・ジュースがありました。
Yoshida: Orenji jūsu ga arimashita.
There was orange juice.

Informal

BETWEEN WOMEN, ONE READING A NEWSPAPER

久江：何かニュースある？
Hisae: Nani ka nyūsu aru?
Is there any news?

朝子：昨日の晩、地震があったって。
Asako: Kinō no ban, jishin ga atta tte.
It says there was an earthquake last night.

Past Tense of *imasu*

> ### *N ga V (imashita).*
>
> N existed.
>
> N = a noun (animate object) acting as the subject of the sentence
>
> V = a verb (*imashita*) in the past tense showing existence

岩佐：何か動物がいましたか。

Iwasa: Nani ka dōbutsu ga imashita ka.

Were there any animals?

川瀬：大きい、茶色の犬がいました。

Kawase: Ōkii, chairo no inu ga imashita.

There was a big brown dog.

BETWEEN MEN

岩佐：何か動物いた。

Iwasa: Nani ka dōbutsu ita.

Were there any animals?

川瀬：いたよ。大きい、茶色の犬がいた。

Kawase: Ita yo. Ōkii, chairo no inu ga ita.

Yes, there was a big brown dog.

Negative Past Tense of *arimasu*

> ### *N ga V (arimasen deshita).*
>
> N didn't exist.
>
> N = a noun (inanimate object) acting as the subject of the sentence

V = a verb (*arimasen deshita*) in the past negative tense showing existence

林：昨日電話がありましたか。

Hayashi: Kinō denwa ga arimashita ka.
Were there any telephone calls yesterday?

野島：いいえ、ありませんでした。

Nojima: Iie, arimasen deshita.
No, there weren't.

BETWEEN WOMEN

貴子：昨日電話あった？

Takako: Kinō denwa atta?
Were there any telephone calls yesterday?

澄江：なかったわよ。

Sumie: Nakatta wa yo.
No, there weren't.

Negative Past Tense of *imasu*

__N__ *ga V (imasen deshita).*

N didn't exist.

N = a noun (animate object) acting as the subject of the sentence

V = a verb (*imasen deshita*) in the past negative tense showing existence

鈴木：昨日係長がいましたか。

Suzuki: Kinō kakari-chō ga imashita ka.
Was the section chief there (here) yesterday?

渡辺：いませんでしたよ。
Watanabe: Imasen deshita yo.
No, he wasn't.

Informal

BETWEEN MEN

鈴木：昨日係長いた？
Suzuki: Kinō kakari-chō ita?
Was the section chief around yesterday?

渡辺：いなかったよ。
Watanabe: Inakatta yo.
No, he wasn't.

Variation **7** Verbs of Existence with Place (*ni*) and Subject

1. **N1** に **N2** が V（あります）。
   N1 ni N2 ga V (arimasu).
   N2 is at (on, in, under, etc.) N1.

   この部屋にコピー機があります。
   Kono heya ni kopī-ki ga arimasu.
   There is a copy machine in this room.

2. **N1**に **N2** が V（います）。
   N1 ni N2 ga V (imasu).
   N2 is at (on, in, under, etc.) N1.

   車の中に友達がいます。
   Kuruma no naka ni tomodachi ga imasu.
   My friend is in the car.

In this variation on Pattern 18 (_N ga V [arimasu/imasu]_), the place where the subject _is_ or _exists_ is indicated. This is done by adding _N1 ni_ to the beginning of the sentence. The same pattern applies to both _arimasu_ and _imasu_, whether in their present or past tenses, polite or informal.

Formula 1

N1 ni N2 ga V (arimasu).

N2 is at (on, in, under, etc.) N1.

N1 = a noun that indicates a location

N2 = a noun (inanimate object) acting as the subject of the sentence

V = a verb (_arimasu_) showing existence

Polite

テーブルの上に牛乳があります。

Tēburu no ue ni gyūnyū ga arimasu.
The milk is on the table.

Informal

BETWEEN MEN

高田：牛乳ある？

Takada: Gyūnyū aru?
Do you have any milk?

岸：あるよ。テーブルの上。

Kishi: Aru yo. Tēburu no ue.
Yes, it's on the table.

In the answer portion of this example, both the subject and _ni_ have been left out for brevity. In addition, the order of the phrase showing location and the verb have been reversed, something that commonly happens in conversation.

N1 ni N2 ga V (imasu).

N2 is at (on, in, under, etc.) N1.

N1 = a noun that indicates a location

N2 = a noun (animate object) acting as the subject of
the sentence

V = a verb (*imasu*) showing existence

Polite

会議室に課長と部長がいます。

Kaigi-shitsu ni kachō to buchō ga imasu.

The section manager and department director are in
the conference room.

Informal

BETWEEN MEN

松本：会議室に誰がいる？

Masumoto: Kaigi-shitsu ni dare ga iru?
Who's in the conference room?

池谷：課長と部長がいるよ。

Iketani: Kachō to buchō ga iru yo.
The section manager and department director.

Variation **8** Verbs of Existence with Subject and Place (*ni*)

1. **N1** は **N2** に V（あります）。

N1 wa N2 ni V (arimasu).

N1 is at (on, in, under, etc.) N2.

その本は机の上にあります。

Sono hon wa tsukue no ue ni arimasu.
That book is on the desk.

2. <u>N1</u> は <u>N2</u> に V（います）。

N1 wa N2 ni V (imasu).

N1 is at (on, in, under, etc.) N2.

猫は家の中にいます。

Neko wa uchi no naka ni imasu.

The cat is in the house.

This variation of Pattern 18 (<u>N</u> *ga V [arimasu/imasu]*) is almost identical in meaning to Variation 7. The difference is that the order of the subject and location have been reversed. In this variation, the subject is emphasized by being placed first in the sentence, whereas in Variation 7 the location was emphasized.

Formula 1

N1 wa N2 ni V (arimasu).

N1 is at (on, in, under, etc.) N2.

N1 = a noun (inanimate object) acting as the subject of the sentence

N2 = a noun that indicates a location

V = a verb (*arimasu*) showing existence

Polite

田中：辞書はどこにありますか。

Tanaka: Jisho wa doko ni arimasu ka.

Where is the dictionary?

青木： 机の上にあります。

Aoki: Tsukue no ue ni arimasu.

It's on the desk.

BETWEEN MEN

田中：辞書、どこにある？
Tanaka: Jisho, doko ni aru?
Where's the dictionary?

青木：机の上。
Aoki: Tsukue no ue.
On the desk.

Notice that the particle *ni* has been dropped after *tsukue no ue,* which is typical of informal speech.

Formula 2

N1 wa N2 ni V (imasu).
N1 is at (on, in, under, etc.) N2.

N1 = a noun (animate object) acting as the subject of the sentence

N2 = a noun that indicates a location

V = a verb (*imasu*) showing existence

Polite

小川：鈴木さんはどこにいますか。
Ogawa: Suzuki-san wa doko ni imasu ka.
Where is Ms. Suzuki?

石山：隣の部屋にいますよ。
Ishiyama: Tonari no heya ni imasu yo.
She's in the next room.

BETWEEN WOMEN

良美：鈴木さんはどこ？
Yoshimi: Suzuki-san wa doko?
Where is Ms. Suzuki?

園子：隣の部屋にいるわ。
Sonoko: Tonari no heya ni iru wa.
She's in the next room.

Basic Patterns 19-22

In this chapter we turn to verbs other than *arimasu* and *imasu*, and we look at them in their past, present, and future tenses. The present and future tenses are both expressed by the *masu* form. Without context, it is impossible to say whether *arukimasu* means "I walk" or "I will walk." In context, it's simple: for example, *Mainichi arukimasu* is "I walk every day," and *Ashita arukimasu* is "I will walk tomorrow." The informal present and future tenses are expressed by the plain form: *aruku*. The negative informal past tense is expressed by the *nakatta* form: *arukanakatta*. (See my *Japanese Verbs at a Glance* for more information about verbs.)

Basic Pattern 19 *V-masu* Sentence in Present/Future Tense

N は V ます。	**私は起きます。**
N wa V-masu.	*Watashi wa okimasu.*
N does V. / N will do V.	I get up. / I will get up.

Here we see the basic pattern of sentences having verbs in the *masu* form (aside from *arimasu* and *imasu*, treated in

Basic Pattern 18). N is the subject of the sentence, and V is the verb telling what the subject does. The *masu* form does not change in conjugation according to the subject of the sentence as happens in English (e.g., "I go," "He goes"). The *masu* form, however, does offer a complication in that it encompasses both present and future tenses; which is relevant must be determined from context.

Formula

***N* wa *V*-masu.**
N does V. / N will do V.
N = a noun acting as the subject of the sentence
V = a verb (predicate) telling what the subject does in the present or future tense

Polite

私は明日の朝7時に起きます。
Watashi wa ashita no asa shichi-ji ni okimasu.
I will get up at 7:00 tomorrow morning.

私はこれから出かけます。
Watashi wa kore kara dekakemasu.
I am going out now.

私は毎日5時半に帰ります。
Watashi wa mainichi goji-han ni kaerimasu.
I go home every day at 5:30.

Informal

MEN

僕、帰る。
Boku, kaeru.
I'm going home.

出かけるよ。
Dekakeru yo.
I'm leaving.

WOMEN

私、帰るわ。
Watashi, kaeru wa.
I'm going home.

私、行くの。
Watashi, iku no.
I'm going.

Variation ① V-*masu* Sentence with *mo* after the Subject

N も V ます。	**私も聞きます。**
N mo V-masu.	*Watashi mo kikimasu.*
N also does V. /	I also listen/hear. /
N also will do V.	I will also listen/hear.

In this variation on Basic Pattern 19 (N *wa* V-*masu*), *wa* is replaced by the particle *mo* ("also"), which modifies the subject. The same thing can be done with the past tense, which is discussed in Variation 4 below.

Formula

N *mo* V-*masu.*
N also does V. / N also will do V.

N = a noun acting as the subject of the sentence

V = a verb (predicate) telling what the subject does in the present or future tense

私も飲みます。

Watashi mo nomimasu.

I also drink. / I also will drink.

私も読みます。

Watashi mo yomimasu.

I also read it. / I also will read it.

山本さんも帰ります。

Yamamoto-san mo kaerimasu.

Mr. Yamamoto also goes home. / Mr. Yamamoto will also go home.

BETWEEN MEN

僕もする。

Boku mo suru.

I'll do it too.

久子も食べるよ。

Hisako mo taberu yo.

Hisako'll eat too.

BETWEEN WOMEN

片山：伊藤さん来る？

Katayama: Itō-san kuru?

Will Mr. Ito come?

小池：来るわよ。森さんも来るわ。

Koike: Kuru wa yo. Mori-san mo kuru wa.

Yes, he'll come. Ms. Mori will too.

N は V ますか。

N wa V-masu ka.

Does N V? /
　Will N V?

後藤さんは行きますか。

Gotō-san wa ikimasu ka.

Does Mr. Goto go? /
　Will Mr. Goto go?

This is a variation on Basic Pattern 19 (*N wa V-masu*). By simply adding *ka* to the end of that pattern, a statement is turned into a question. The same thing can be done with the past tense, which is discussed in Variation 4 below.

Formula

N wa V-masu ka.

Does N V? / Will N V?

N = a noun acting as the subject of the sentence

V = a verb (predicate) telling what the subject does in the present or future tense

ka = a particle indicating a question

Polite

児島さんは食べますか。

Kojima-san wa tabemasu ka.

Will Mr. Kojima eat?

沢井さんは歩きますか。

Sawai-san wa arukimasu ka.

Will Mr. Sawai walk?

BETWEEN MEN

古賀：帰る？

Koga: Kaeru?

You going home?

笠井：うん、帰るよ。小野君は？

Kasai: Un, kaeru yo. Ono-kun wa?

Yes, I'm leaving. What about Ono?

古賀：もう帰ったよ。

Koga: Mō kaetta yo.

He left already.

Variation 3 — *V-masu* Sentence in the Negative

N は V ません。	**私は起きません。**
N wa V-masen.	*Watashi wa okimasen.*
N does not V. /	I do not get up. /
N will not V.	I will not get up.

This variation presents a negative statement. It is formed by replacing *masu* in Basic Pattern 19 (*N wa V-masu*) with *masen*. As with Pattern 19, the variation represents both present and future tenses, which are distinguished by context. Note that this pattern can also be applied to Variations 1–2 above. The past negative is formed by adding *deshita* after *masen*.

Formula

N wa V-masen.

N does not V. / N will not V.

N = a noun acting as the subject of the sentence

V = a verb (predicate) telling what the subject does (or, in this case, does not do) in the present or future tense

私は飲みません。
Watashi wa nomimasen.
I do not drink. / I will not drink.

私は出かけません。
Watashi wa dekakemasen.
I do not go out. / I will not go out.

Informal

BETWEEN MEN

小池：これ買う？
Koike: Kore kau?
Are you going to buy it?
緒方：僕、買わない。
Ogata: Boku, kawanai.
No, I'm not.

Informal

BETWEEN WOMEN

岡田：今日行く？
Okada: Kyō iku?
Are you going today?
黒田：私、行かないわ。
Kuroda: Watashi, ikanai wa.
No, I'm not.

N は V ました。

N wa V-mashita.

N did V.

私は酔いました。

Watashi wa yoimashita.

I got drunk.

This variation is the past tense of Basic Pattern 19 (<u>N</u> wa <u>V</u>-*masu*). It is formed by replacing *masu* with *mashita*.

Formula

<u>N</u> wa <u>V</u>-*mashita.*

N did V.

N = a noun acting as the subject of the sentence

V = a past-tense verb (predicate) telling what the subject did

Polite

私は行きました。

Watashi wa ikimashita.

I went.

私は出かけました。

Watashi wa dekakemashita.

I went out.

私は帰りました。

Watashi wa kaerimashita.

I went home. / I left.

BETWEEN MEN

僕、食べたよ。
Boku, tabeta yo.
I ate.

山田君出かけたよ。
Yamada-kun dekaketa yo.
Yamada went out.

BETWEEN WOMEN

私、見たわ。
Watashi, mita wa.
I saw it.

私、買ったのよ。
Watashi, katta no yo.
I bought it.

Basic Pattern **20** Time Indicated by *ni*

<u>N1</u> は <u>N2</u> に <u>V</u>ます。
N1 wa N2 ni V-masu.
N1 does V at N2. / N1 will do V at N2.

私は7時に起きます。
Watashi wa shichi-ji ni okimasu.
I get up at 7:00. / I will get up at 7:00.

This pattern shows the time at which something habitually takes place ("I get up at 7:00") or will take place ("I will get up at 7:00"). If you wish to indicate the time when something occurred in the past, you can combine *N2 ni* in this pattern with Basic Pattern 19, Variation 4.

Formula

N1 wa N2 ni V-masu.
N1 does V at N2. / N1 will do V at N2.
N1 = a noun acting as the subject of the sentence
N2 = a noun indicating the time at which an action takes place or will take place
V = a verb in the present or future tense

Polite

私は7時に起きます。
Watashi wa shichi-ji ni okimasu.
I get up at 7:00. / I will get up at 7:00.

私は8時に出かけます。
Watashi wa hachi-ji ni dekakemasu.
I leave at 8:00. / I will leave at 8:00.

私は6時に戻ります。
Watashi wa roku-ji ni modorimasu.
I return at 6:00. / I will return at 6:00.

Informal

BETWEEN WOMEN

佳枝：いつ出かけるの？
Yoshie: Itsu dekakeru no?
When are you leaving?

宏美：来週よ。
Hiromi: Raishū yo.
Next week.

BETWEEN MEN

和夫：いつ行く？

Kazuo: Itsu iku?

When will you go?

正二：明日。

Shōji: Ashita.

Tomorrow.

As you can see from the above, if you wish to ask when someone did, does, or will do something, you can add the words *itsu* ("when") or *nan-ji ni* ("at what time") to the beginning of the question.

Basic Pattern **21** Direction of Movement Indicated by *ni/e*

<u>N1</u> は <u>N2</u> へ/に <u>V</u> ます。

N1 wa N2 e/ni V-masu.

N1 goes to N2. / N1 will go to N2.

私は会社へ/に行きます。

Watashi wa kaisha e/ni ikimasu.

I go to the office. / I will go to the office.

In this pattern, movement is taking place from one place to another. The place toward which the movement is directed is indicated by *e/ni*. The verb is usually the Japanese equivalent of "go," "come," "return," or some similar word. In this simple pattern the particles *e* and *ni* are interchangeable, but in the example sentences below we have not repeatedly indicated this fact. The *N2 e/ni* pattern can also be used in the past tense.

<u>N1 wa <u>N2</u> e/ni <u>V-masu</u>.</u>

N1 goes to N2. / N1 will go to N2.

N1 = a noun acting as the subject of the sentence

N2 = a noun indicating a place toward which the subject is moving

V = a verb (predicate) indicating movement from one place to another

Polite

明日阿部さんは銀座へ行きます。

Ashita Abe-san wa Ginza e ikimasu.

Mr. Abe is going to Ginza tomorrow.

岸さんは学校に帰りました。

Kishi-san wa gakkō ni kaerimashita.

Mr. Kishi returned to school.

Informal

BETWEEN MEN

太郎：今日、出かける？

Tarō: Kyō, dekakeru?

You going out today?

次郎：うん、大学へ行くよ。

Jirō: Un, daigaku e iku yo.

Yes, I'm going to the university.

Variation 1 Time (*ni*) and Movement (*ni/e*)

<u>N1</u>は <u>N2</u> に <u>N3</u> へ / に <u>V</u> ます。

N1 wa N2 ni N3 e/ni V-masu.

N1 goes to N3 at N2. / N1 will go to N3 at N2.

私は8時に会社へ行きます。

Watashi wa hachi-ji ni kaisha e ikimasu.

I go to the office at 8:00. / I will go to the office at 8:00.

This variation is a combination of Basic Patterns 20 (*N1 wa N2 ni V-masu*) and 21 (*N1 wa N2 e/ni V-masu*), which offer formulas for indicating time and place. The verb should indicate movement from one place to another. The formula in this pattern can also be used with verbs in the past tense.

Formula

N1 wa N2 ni N3 e/ni V-masu.

N1 goes to N3 at N2. / N1 will go to N3 at N2.

N1 = a noun acting as the subject of the sentence

N2 = a noun indicating the time at which an action takes place or will take place

N3 = a noun indicating a place toward which the subject is moving

V = a verb (predicate) indicating movement from one place to another

Polite

私は日曜日に教会へ行きます。

Watashi wa nichiyōbi ni kyōkai e ikimasu.

I go to church on Sundays. / I will go to church on Sunday.

Notice that, without context, the example above is capable of two interpretations, whereas the one immediately below is capable of only one reasonable interpretation, since we can't imagine the prime minister going to the United States every Monday.

首相は月曜日にアメリカへ行きます。

Shushō wa getsuyōbi ni Amerika e ikimasu.
The prime minister will go to the United States on Monday.

遠藤さんは午前6時に飛行場へ来ました。

Endō-san wa gozen roku-ji ni hikō-jō e kimashita.
Mr. Endo came to the airport at 6:00 A.M.

Informal

BETWEEN WOMEN

古賀：明日のパーティ、何時に行く？

Koga: Ashita no pāti, nan-ji ni iku?
What time will you go to tomorrow's party?

岡本：7時ごろ行く。

Okamoto: Shichi-ji goro iku.
I'm going around 7:00.

Basic Pattern **22** Direct Object Indicated by *o*

N1 は N2 を V ます。	**私は映画を見ます。**
N1 wa N2 o V-masu.	*Watashi wa eiga o mimasu.*
N1 V's / will V N2.	I watch movies. /
	I will watch a movie.

In this pattern the verb is a transitive verb, which means that it takes an object. The object is followed by the particle *o*, which indicates that the word is on the receiving end of an action. (The particle *o* has other uses as well.)

<u>*N1*</u> *wa* <u>*N2*</u> *o* <u>*V-masu.*</u>

N1 V's / will V N2.

N1 = a noun acting as the subject of the sentence

N2 = a noun (object) that receives the action of a verb

V = a transitive verb; i.e., a verb that requires an object to complete its intended meaning

菊池さんはよく寿司を食べます。

Kikuchi-san wa yoku sushi o tabemasu.

Mr. Kikuchi often eats sushi.

私は昨日の晩家でテレビを見ました。

Watashi wa kinō no ban uchi de terebi o mimashita.

Last night I watched television at home.

大西さんは先週鞄を買いました。

Ōnishi-san wa senshū kaban o kaimashita.

Ms. Onishi bought a handbag last week.

WOMEN AT A RESTAURANT

笠井：江口さんは今日何食べるの？

Kasai: Eguchi-san wa kyō nani taberu no?

Ms. Eguchi, what are you going to eat today?

江口：私はてんぷらを食べるわ。岩崎さんは？

Eguchi: Watashi wa tempura o taberu wa. Iwasaki-san wa?

I'll have tempura. How about you, Ms. Iwasaki?

岩崎：私はお寿司がいいわ。

Iwasaki: Watashi wa osushi ga ii wa.

Sushi is best for me.

MOTHER AND CHILD

母親：薬、飲んだ？
Hahaoya: Kusuri, nonda?
Mother: Have you taken your medicine?

子供：もう飲んだよ。
Kodomo: Mō nonda yo.
Child: Yes, I already did.

母親：いつ飲んだの？
Hahaoya: Itsu nonda no?
Mother: When did you take it?

子供：今朝飲んだ。
Kodomo: Kesa nonda.
Child: I took it this morning.

◖ Variation ❶ Direct Object (*o*) and Location (*de*) ◗

N1 は N2 で N3 を V ます。
N1 wa N2 de N3 o V-masu.
N1 V's / will V N3 at N2.

私は家で晩御飯を食べます。
Watashi wa uchi de ban-gohan o tabemasu.
I eat / will eat supper at home.

In this variation, another element has been added to Basic Pattern 22 (*N1 wa N2 o V-masu*): the place where an action occurs. This is indicated by *de*, which is obviously different from the indication of place that occurs in Basic Pattern 21 (*N1 wa N2 e/ni V-masu*) since the latter shows the place toward which movement takes place.

N1 wa N2 de N3 o V-masu.

N1 V's / will V N3 at N2.

N1 = a noun acting as the subject of the sentence

N2 = a noun indicating where action takes place

N3 = a noun (object) that receives the action of a verb

V = a transitive verb; i.e., a verb that requires an object to complete its intended meaning

私は自分の部屋でテレビを見ます。

Watashi wa jibun no heya de terebi o mimasu.

I watch television in my own room.

広谷さんは大学のコートでテニスをします。

Hirotani-san wa daigaku no kōto de tenisu o shimasu.

Mr. Hirotani plays tennis on the university court.

山本：トムさんは、よくテレビを見ますか。

Yamamoto: Tomu-san wa, yoku terebi o mimasu ka.

Tom, do you watch television much?

トム：ええ、寮でよくドラマを見ます。

Tomu: Ee, ryō de yoku dorama o mimasu.

Yes, I often watch TV dramas at the dorm.

BETWEEN MEN

山本：トムは、テレビを見る？

Yamamoto: Tomu wa, terebi o miru?

Tom, do you watch television?

トム：うん、寮でよくドラマを見るよ。

Tomu: Un, ryō de yoku dorama o miru yo.

Yes, I watch TV dramas at the dorm.

> **Variation ❷** Time (*ni*), Location (*de*), and Direct Object (*o*)
>
> ## <u>N1</u> は <u>N2</u> に <u>N3</u> で <u>N4</u> を <u>V</u> ます。
>
> *N1 wa N2 ni N3 de N4 o V-masu.*
>
> N1 V's / will V N4 at N2 in N3.
>
> ## 私は毎朝9時に会社で仕事を始めます。
>
> *Watashi wa maiasa ku-ji ni kaisha de shigoto o hajime-masu.*
>
> Every morning at 9:00 I start work at the office.

In this variation of Variation 1 (*<u>N1</u> wa <u>N2</u> de <u>N3</u> o <u>V</u>-masu*), the element of time as given in Basic Pattern 20 (*<u>N1</u> wa <u>N2</u> ni <u>V</u>-masu*) is added. In all, we have the time at which an action takes place (*N2 ni*), where it takes place (*N3 de*), and the object of the verb (i.e., what is done; *N4 o*).

Formula

<u>N1</u> wa <u>N2</u> ni <u>N3</u> de <u>N4</u> o <u>V</u>-masu.

N1 V's / will V N4 at N2 in N3.

N1 = a noun acting as the subject of the sentence

N2 = a noun indicating the time at which an action takes place or will take place

N3 = a noun indicating where action takes place

N4 = a noun (object) that receives the action of a verb

V = a transitive verb; i.e., a verb that requires an object to complete its intended meaning

首相は15日に国会で演説をします。

Shushō wa jūgo-nichi ni kokkai de enzetsu o shimasu.

The prime minister will make a speech in the Diet on the 15th.

森本：営業会議はどうしますか。

Morimoto: Eigyō-kaigi wa dō shimasu ka.

What are we doing about the sales meeting?

吉田：月末に会議室でミーティングをします。

Yoshida: Getsumatsu ni kaigi-shitsu de mītingu o shimasu.

At the end of the month a meeting will be held in the conference room.

BETWEEN WOMEN

宏美：お昼は何時頃、どこで食べる？

Hiromi: Ohiru wa nanji goro, doko de taberu?

When and where shall we have lunch?

佐和子：銀座で1時頃食べない？

Sawako: Ginza de ichi-ji goro tabenai?

Shall we eat at Ginza about 1:00?

In the first part of this last example, notice that the object (*ohiru*) of the verb *taberu* has become the topic of the sentence. Further, neither *nanji goro* nor *ichi-ji goro* is followed by *ni*. The use of *ni* after *goro* is standard practice, but particularly in casual conversation *ni* can be dropped, with only a slight loss in emphasis on the time being indicated.

<u>N1</u> は <u>N2</u> を <u>V1</u> に <u>V2</u> ます。

N1 wa N2 o V1 ni V2-masu.

N1 V2's / will V2 in order to V1 N2.

私は歌舞伎を見に行きます。

Watashi wa kabuki o mi ni ikimasu.

I go to see Kabuki. ／ I will go to see Kabuki.

In this variation of Basic Pattern 22 (<u>*N1*</u> *wa* <u>*N2*</u> *o* <u>*V*</u>-*masu*), V1 shows the purpose of V2 (i.e., one will *go* [V2] in order to *see* [V1]). V1 is in the *masu* stem form: that is, what remains of a verb in the *masu* form after *masu* has been removed (e.g., *mi-masu* becomes *mi*). The *masu* stem is followed by the particle *ni* and a verb in past, present, or future tense. The final verb is often *iku* ("go"), *kuru* ("come"), *dekakeru* ("go out"), or other verbs showing movement from one place to another.

Formula

<u>*N1*</u> *wa* <u>*N2*</u> *o* <u>*V1*</u> *ni* <u>*V2*</u>-*masu*.

N1 V2's / will V2 in order to V1 N2.

N1 = a noun acting as the subject of the sentence

N2 = a noun (object) that receives the action of a verb

V1 = a transitive verb in the *masu* stem form

ni = a particle that indicates purpose

V2 = a verb (predicate) indicating movement from one place to another

私はテニスをしに行きます。

Watashi wa tenisu o shi ni ikimasu.

I go to play tennis. / I will go to play tennis.

私は週末軽井沢へテニスをしに行きます。

Watashi wa shūmatsu Karuizawa e tenisu o shi ni ikimasu.

This weekend I will go to Karuizawa to play tennis.

Informal

BETWEEN MEN

康夫：土曜日、予定ある？

Yasuo: Doyōbi, yotei aru?

Do you have any plans for Saturday?

孝義：朝6時に千葉へゴルフをしに出かけるよ。

Takayoshi: Asa roku-ji ni Chiba e gorufu o shi ni dekakeru yo.

I'm leaving for Chiba at 6:00 in the morning to play golf.

Basic Patterns 23-27

This chapter will principally look at the *te* form of verbs when followed by a sentence-ending verb. The sentence-ending verb can be *arimasu* or *imasu* or another verb in the *masu* form, or their informal equivalents. The patterns discussed here cover a great deal of territory, from action in progress, repeated action, successive actions to requests and prohibitions.

Basic Pattern 23 *Te imasu* Showing Action in Progress

N は V ています。
N wa V-te imasu.
N is doing V.

太郎はテレビを見ています。
Tarō wa terebi o mite imasu.
Taro is watching television.

This pattern indicates that an action carried out by the subject of the sentence is now in progress. Variations on this pattern (treated below) deal with regular or habitual actions and continued states rather than actions per se.

<u>N</u> wa <u>V</u>-te imasu.
N is doing V.
N = a noun acting as the subject of the sentence
V = a *te* form plus *imasu* indicating that an action is in progress

松本さんは今本を読んでいます。

Matsumoto-san wa ima hon o yonde imasu.
Mr. Matsumoto is reading a book now.

小原さんは今音楽を聴いています。

Ohara-san wa ima ongaku o kiite imasu.
Mr. Ohara is listening to music now.

小松：福田さんはいますか。

Komatsu: Fukuda-san wa imasu ka.
Komatsu: Is Mr. Fukuda there?

伊東：福田さんは今電話をかけています。

Itō: Fukuda-san wa ima denwa o kakete imasu.
Mr. Fukuda is making a telephone call right now.

小松：小原さんはいま何してる？

Komatsu: Ohara-san wa ima nani shite 'ru?
What's Ms. Ohara doing now?

伊東：小原さんは今音楽を聴いている。

Itō: Ohara-san wa ima ongaku o kiite iru.
Ms. Ohara is listening to music right now.

田中：福田さんいる？

Tanaka: Fukuda-san iru?
Is Mr. Fukuda there?

鈴木：福田さんは今電話をかけているよ。

Suzuki: Fukuda-san wa ima denwa o kakete iru yo.

Mr. Fukuda's making a call right now.

◀ Variation ▶ **1** ▷ *Te imasu* **Showing Regular or Habitual Action**

<u>N</u> は <u>V</u> ています。

N wa V-te imasu.

N is doing/does V (on a regular basis).

富田さんは航空会社に勤めています。

Tomita-san wa kōkū-gaisha ni tsutomete imasu.

Mr. Tomita works for an airline company.

In this variation on Basic Pattern 23 (<u>N</u> *wa* <u>V</u>-*te imasu*), the pattern itself is the same as the Basic Pattern, as well as Variation 2 below, but the meaning is slightly different. Whereas in Basic Pattern 23 the action is actually ongoing, in this variation the action is regular or habitual over a relatively lengthy period of time, such as "working" for a company, "living" in a certain place, or "attending" a health club on a frequent basis.

◀ Formula ▶ ─────────────────────

<u>N</u> *wa* <u>V</u>-*te imasu.*

N is doing/does V (on a regular basis).

N = a noun acting as the subject of the sentence

V = a *te* form plus *imasu* indicating that an action is being carried out on a regular basis over a relatively long period of time

吉田：山田さんはどこに勤めていますか。

Yoshida: Yamada-san wa doko ni tsutomete imasu ka.

Where does Mr. Yamada work?

栗山：山田さんは銀行に勤めています。

Kuriyama: Yamada-san wa ginkō ni tsutomete imasu.

Mr. Yamada works for a bank.

吉田：そうですか？今どこに住んでいますか。

Yoshida: Sō desu ka? Ima doko ni sunde imasu ka.

Is that so? Where does he live?

栗山：神戸に住んでいます。

Kuriyama: Kōbe ni sunde imasu.

He lives in Kobe.

BETWEEN WOMEN

吉田：山田さん、どこに勤めているの？

Yoshida: Yamada-san, doko ni tsutomete iru no?

Where does Mr. Yamada work?

栗山：銀行に勤めているわよ。

Kuriyama: Ginkō ni tsutomete iru wa yo.

He works for a bank.

吉田：そう？今どこに住んでるの？

Yoshida: Sō? Ima doko ni sunde 'ru no?

Is that so? Where does he live?

栗山：神戸に住んでるわよ。

Kuriyama: Kōbe ni sunde 'ru wa yo.

He lives in Kobe.

<u>N</u> は <u>V</u> ています。

N wa V-te imasu.

N is in the condition of V.

雪はいまでも積もっています。

Yuki wa ima demo tsumotte imasu.

There is snow on the ground even now.

In this variation on Basic Pattern 23 (<u>N</u> *wa* <u>V</u>-*te imasu*), the pattern itself is the same as the Basic Pattern, as well as Variation 1, but the meaning is slightly different. This variation expresses a state or condition, which means that a certain action has taken place and the result of that action is still in effect. For example, "Snow fell on the ground" would be the action, and "There is still snow on the ground" would be the resulting condition or state. The *te*-form verb used in this pattern should be an intransitive verb: i.e., a verb that does not take a direct object (a noun followed by *o*). See my *Japanese Verbs at a Glance* for information about transitive and intransitive verbs.

Formula

<u>N</u> *wa* <u>V</u>-*te imasu.*

N is in the condition of V.

N = a noun acting as the subject of the sentence

V = a *te*-form intransitive verb plus *imasu* indicating the condition that has resulted from a certain action

ヘレン：東京の電車はいつも混んでいますか。
Heren: Tōkyō no densha wa itsumo konde imasu ka.
Are Tokyo trains always crowded?

野上：朝と夕方は混んでいますよ。
Nogami: Asa to yūgata wa konde imasu yo.
They're crowded in the mornings and evenings.

林：窓があいていますね。
Hayashi: Mado ga aite imasu ne.
The window is open, I see.

横田：風であいたんでしょう。
Yokota: Kaze de aita 'n deshō.
It was probably the wind that blew it open.

BETWEEN WOMEN

ヘレン：東京の電車，いつも混んでる？
Heren: Tōkyō no densha, itsumo konde 'ru?
Are Tokyo trains always crowded?

野上：朝と夕方は混んでるわ。
Nogami: Asa to yūgata wa konde 'ru wa.
They're crowded in the mornings and evenings.

BETWEEN MEN

林：窓があいてるね。
Hayashi: Mado ga aite 'ru ne.
I see the window is open.

横田：風であいたんだろう。

Yokota: Kaze de aita 'n darō.

It was probably the wind.

<u>N</u>が<u>V</u>てあります。

N ga V-te arimasu.

N has been put in the state of V.

部屋の電気がつけてあります。

Heya no denki ga tsukete arimasu.

The lights in the room have been turned on.

This variation on Basic Pattern 23 (<u>N</u> *wa* <u>V</u>-te imasu) is the same as Variation 2 in that it expresses a state or condition that is the result of a certain action. It is different in that the action that produces the condition was done deliberately, not unintentionally as by natural forces or random human actions. Further, the *te*-form verb should be a transitive verb (one than can take an object in the *N o* form), and it should be followed by *arimasu* rather than *imasu*.

Formula

<u>N</u> *ga* <u>V</u>-te arimasu.

N has been put in the state of V.

N = a noun acting as the subject of the sentence

V = a *te*-form transitive verb plus *arimasu* indicating the condition that has resulted from an intentional action

秘書：会議の準備ができています。

Hisho: Kaigi no junbi ga dekite imasu.

Secretary: Everything is ready for the meeting.

加藤：書類や飲みものは用意してありますか。

Katō: Shorui ya nomimono wa yōi shite arimasu ka.

Kato: Are the documents and drinks ready?

秘書：はい、書類は机の上に並べてあります。 飲み物も用意してあります。

Hisho: Hai, shorui wa tsukue no ue ni narabete arimasu. Nomimono mo yōi shite arimasu.

Secretary: Yes, the papers are on the table. The drinks are also ready.

BETWEEN MOTHER AND DAUGHTER

母：もうすぐお客様がいらっしゃるけど、お 湯沸かしてある？

Haha: Mō sugu okyaku-sama ga irassharu kedo, oyu wakashite aru?

Mother: The guests will be arriving soon. Have you boiled the water?

娘：ええ、コーヒーカップも出してあるわ。

Musume: Ee, kōhī kappu mo dashite aru wa.

Daughter: Yes, and the coffee cups have also been put out. / Yes, the cups are also ready.

Basic Pattern **24** *Te* Form Indicating Successive Actions

N は V1 て、 V2 て、 V3 ます。

N wa V1-te, V2-te, V3-masu.

N does V1, V2, and V3.

> **太郎は朝御飯を食べて、新聞を読んで、会社
> へ行きます。**
>
> *Tarō wa asa-gohan o tabete, shinbun o yonde, kaisha e
> ikimasu.*
>
> Taro eats breakfast, reads the newspaper, and goes to
> the office.

This pattern shows several actions (indicated by verbs in
the *te* form) that are being carried out one after the other. The
actions are not in random order but in the order of occur-
rence. Since the *te* form does not express tense in itself, the
tense is decided by the sentence-ending verb. It is usual for
this pattern to occur with two or three *te*-form verbs.

Formula

_N_ wa _V1-te, V2-te, V3-masu._

N does V1, V2, and V3.

N = a noun acting as the subject of the sentence

V1 = a verb in the *te* form

V2 = a verb in the *te* form

V3 = a verb in the *masu* (or *mashita,* for the past tense)
form, which decides the tense of the whole sentence

Polite

島田：日曜日は何をしましたか。

Shimada: Nichiyōbi wa nani o shimashita ka.

What did you do on Sunday?

松本：友達と六本木へ行って、食事をして、
映画を見ました。

*Matsumoto: Tomodachi to Roppongi e itte, shokuji o shite,
eiga o mimashita.*

I went to Roppongi with a friend, ate, and saw a movie.

BETWEEN WOMEN

緑：箱根、楽しかった？

Midori: Hakone, tanoshikatta?

Was Hakone fun?

祐子：バスで芦ノ湖へ行って、遊覧船に乗っ
たの。気持ちよかったわ。

Yuko: Basu de Ashi no ko e itte, yūran-sen ni notta no. Kimochi yokatta wa.

We went to Lake Ashi by bus and took a sightseeing boat. It felt great.

Variation 1 *Te kara for One Action Occurring after Another*

N は V1 てから V2 ます。

N wa V1-te kara V2-masu.

N does / will do V2 after V1.

太郎は朝起きてからシャワーを浴びます。

Tarō wa asa okite kara shawā o abimasu.

Taro takes a shower after he gets up.

The difference between this variation and Basic Pattern 24 (*N wa V1-te, V2-te, V3-masu*) is that while the basic pattern shows several actions occurring one after another, this variation notes specifically that one action occurs after another. This is accomplished by the use of a *te* form followed by the particle *kara* ("after"). Since the *te* form does not indicate tense, that is determined by the verb that ends the sentence.

<u>N</u> wa <u>V1</u>-te kara <u>V2</u>-masu.

N does / will do V2 after V1.

N = a noun acting as the subject of the sentence

V1 = a verb in the *te* form

kara = a particle meaning "after," which indicates that the action of the *te*-form verb precedes that of the sentence-ending verb

V2 = a sentence-ending verb that determines the tense of the *te*-form verb and the sentence as a whole

立花：昨日家へ帰ってから何をしましたか。

Tachibana: Kinō uchi e kaette kara nani o shimashita ka.

What did you do after you went home yesterday?

小林：帰ってからすぐ寝ましたよ。

Kobayashi: Kaette kara sugu nemashita yo.

I went to bed soon after I got home.

BETWEEN WOMEN

晴美：その本面白かった？

Harumi: Sono hon omoshirokatta?

Was that book interesting?

喜美子：とっても良かった。読んでから私の人生観が変わったわ。

Kimiko: Tottemo yokatta. Yonde kara watashi no jinsei-kan ga kawatta wa.

Yes, very good. My outlook on life changed after reading it.

<u>N</u> は <u>V1</u> 前に <u>V2</u> ます。

N wa V1 mae ni V2-masu.

N does / will do V2 before V1.

私は家へ帰る前に買い物をします。

Watashi wa uchi e kaeru mae ni kaimono o shimasu.

I shop before I go home. / I will do some shopping before going home.

The difference between this variation and Basic Pattern 24 (*N wa V1-te, V2-te, V3-masu*) is that while the basic pattern shows several actions occurring one after another, this variation notes specifically that one action occurs before another. This is accomplished by the use of a plain-form verb followed by the noun-particle combination *mae ni* ("before"). Since the plain-form verb is not taken as indicating tense, that is determined by the verb that ends the sentence.

Formula

N wa <u>V1</u> mae ni <u>V2</u>-masu.

N does / will do V2 before V1.

N = a noun acting as the subject of the sentence

V1 = a verb in the plain form

mae ni = a combination of the noun *mae* ("before") with the particle *ni* (indicating the time at which something occurs)

V2 = a sentence-ending verb that determines the tense of the plain-form verb preceding *mae ni* as well as the tense of the sentence as a whole

小林：雨が降り出す前に着きたいですね。

Kobayashi: Ame ga furidasu mae ni tsukitai desu ne.

I hope we can get there before it starts raining.

竹内：降る前に着きますよ。

Takeuchi: Furu mae ni tsukimasu yo.

I'm sure we can get there before the rain starts.

Note that in the first sentence of this two-sentence dialogue the subject for the plain-form verb is different from that of the sentence-ending verb (the subject of this verb, which has been omitted as being understood, would be *watashi-tachi ga*). In the second sentence of this dialogue, both subjects have been omitted as being understood from context.

Informal

BETWEEN WOMEN

香織：いつお風呂にはいるの？

Kaori: Itsu ofuro ni hairu no?

When do you take your bath?

幸恵：毎晩寝る前にはいる。

Sachie: Maiban neru mae ni hairu.

I take one every night before going to bed.

Basic Pattern 25 | *Te kudasai* for a Polite Request

Vてください。	本を見せてください。
V-te kudasai.	*Hon o misete kudasai.*
Please do V.	Please show me the book.

This pattern is used for making direct requests or asking favors, with a *te*-form verb indicating what is requested. Although the sentence-ending verb is in the form of a command, it is makes use of the polite *kudasaru* and therefore represents a polite request, not an order. The subject (*anata wa*) is always omitted.

‹ Formula ›

_V_-te kudasai.
Please do V.

V = a *te*-form verb indicating the nature of the request or favor asked

kudasai = "please give me"; the command form of *kuda-saru* ("to give," with the giver being shown respect and the receiver seen as a beneficiary of the action)

‹ Polite ›

課長：この書類を部長に渡してください。
Kachō: Kono shorui o buchō ni watashite kudasai.

Section manager: Please give these papers to the department director.

秘書：はい、わかりました。
Hisho: Hai, wakarimashita.

Secretary: Certainly.

‹ Informal ›

BETWEEN WOMEN

友子：この手紙、弘子に渡して。
Tomoko: Kono tegami, Hiroko ni watashite.

Tomoko: Please give this letter to Hiroko.

敏子：いいね。

Toshiko: Ii wa.

Toshiko: O.K.

In the informal version of this pattern, the polite *kudasai* is dropped, and the sentence ends with a *te*-form verb, which is sufficient in itself to make a casual request or ask a favor.

Variation **1**	*Nai de kudasai* for a Negative Polite Request

<u>V</u> ないでください。

V-nai de kudasai.

Please don't do V.

ここでたばこを吸わないでください。

Koko de tabako o suwanai de kudasai.

Please don't smoke here.

In this variation of Basic Pattern 25 (<u>V</u>-*te kudasai*), the *te*-form verb is transformed into its negative equivalent: i.e., a *nai*-form verb followed by *de*. Here the speaker is requesting that something not be done. As in the basic pattern, the subject is not mentioned since it is assumed to be "you," that is, the party being addressed.

Formula

<u>V</u>-*nai de kudasai.*

Please don't do V.

V-*nai de* = a verb in the plain negative (*nai*) form followed by *de*; this may be considered the negative form of a *te*-form verb

kudasai = "please give me"; the command form of

182   Verb Sentences

kudasaru ("to give," with the giver being shown respect and the receiver seen as a beneficiary of the action)

この建物の前に車を止めないでください。

Kono tatemono no mae ni kuruma o tomenai de kudasai.
Please don't park your car in front of this building.

バスの中で携帯電話を使わないでください。

Basu no naka de keitai-denwa o tsukawanai de kudasai.
Please don't use your cellular phone inside the bus.

BETWEEN WOMEN

姉：今電話使わないで。

Ane: Ima denwa tsukawanai de.
Older sister: Don't use the telephone right now.

妹：どうして？

Imōto: Dōshite?
Younger sister: How come?

姉：友達がもうすぐ電話してくるの。

Ane: Tomodachi ga mō sugu denwa shite kuru no.
Older sister: A friend will be calling any minute now.

As we can see from this example, the informal version of this variation drops the polite *kudasai*, and the sentence ends with a verb in the plain negative (*nai*) form followed by *de*, which is sufficient in itself to make a casual request or ask a favor of this sort.

V てくださいませんか。

V-te kudasaimasen ka.

Would you please do V?

本を見せてくださいませんか？

Hon o misete kudasaimasen ka?

Would you please show me the book?

In this variation of Basic Pattern 25 (*V-te kudasai*), the sentence-ending verb has been made into a negative question (*kudasaimasen ka*, meaning roughly "Wouldn't you give…?"). By this means, the request is made more polite than in the basic pattern.

Formula

V-te kudasaimasen ka.

Would you please do V?

V = a *te*-form verb indicating the nature of the request or favor asked

kudasaimasen ka = the negative *masu* form of the verb *kudasaru* ("to give," with the giver being shown respect and the receiver seen as a beneficiary of the action); the addition of the particle *ka* creates a question

Polite

秘書：すみませんが、社長に電話をしてくださいませんか。

Hisho: Sumimasen ga, shachō ni denwa o shite kudasaimasen ka.

Secretary: Would you please call the president?

部長：ああ、いいよ。

Buchō: Ah, ii yo.

Department director: O.K.

As seen in the example that follows, this variation can also be used to make a request that something not be done. The result is a somewhat more polite version of Variation 1 above.

ここに駐車をしないでくださいませんか。

Koko ni chūsha o shinai de kudasaimasen ka.

Would you please not park here?

| Variation **3** | *Te itadakemasen ka* **for a Polite Request** |

V ていただけませんか。

V-te itadakemasen ka.

Would you mind doing V?

電話番号を教えていただけませんか。

Denwa bangō o oshiete itadakemasen ka.

Would you mind telling me your phone number?

In this variation of Basic Pattern 25 (*V-te kudasai*), *kudasai* has been replaced by *itadakemasen ka* (roughly, "Could I receive …?"). As with the basic pattern, it is preceded by a *te*-form verb that indicates the nature of the request or favor being asked. The politeness level of this variation may be considered as being just slightly above that of Variation 2 (*V-te kudasaimasen ka*). It is similar to the basic pattern and to the other variations in that the *te*-form verb may appear in its negative form (*nai de*) and the subject of the verb is not expressed.

V-te itadakemasen ka.

Would you mind doing V?

V = a *te*-form verb indicating the nature of the request or favor asked

itadakemasen ka = lit., "could I humbly receive"; the negative *masu* form of *itadaku* (*itadakimasen*) has been made into its negative potential form (indicating ability, or whether one *can* do something): *itadakemasen*. The sentence-ending *ka* converts the whole into a question: "Could I possibly receive …?"

Polite

すみませんが、ご住所を書いていただけませんか。

Sumimasen ga, gojūsho o kaite itadakemasen ka.

I hate to put you to any trouble, but would you mind writing down your address?

申し訳ありませんが、ここでたばこを吸わないでいただけませんか。

Mōshiwake arimasen ga, koko de tabako o suwanai de itadakemasen ka.

I hate to be a bother, but would you please refrain from smoking here.

Variation 4 *Te hoshii for a Request*

V て欲しいんですが。

V-te hoshii 'n desu ga.

I would like to have V.

この時計を直して欲しいんですが。

Kono tokei o naoshite hoshii 'n desu ga.

I would like to have this watch fixed.

In this variation of Basic Pattern 25 (*V-te kudasai*), *kudasai* has been replaced by *hoshii* ("like to have …"). As in the other variations under this pattern, the *te*-form verb indicates the nature of the request being made or the favor being asked. This variation is distinguished by the fact that the sentence ends in *ga* ("but"). *Ga* may be seen here as a means of softening the request by suggesting that there may be circumstances that would prevent one's wish from being fulfilled. This pattern, along with *te moraitai 'n desu ga*, is often used when addressing store clerks, bellhops, and others working in service capacities.

Formula

V-te hoshii 'n desu ga.

I would like to have V.

V = a *te*-form verb indicating the nature of the request or favor asked

hoshii 'n desu ga = lit., "would like to have … but": indicating that one would like to have something done but realizes, at least as a form of politeness, that there may be contrary circumstances

Polite

客：これを家に届けて欲しいんですが……

Kyaku: Kore o uchi ni todokete hoshi 'n desu ga …

A customer: I'd like to have this delivered.

店員：はい、かしこまりました。

Ten'in: Hai, kashikomarimashita.

Clerk: I understand.

Basic Pattern　26　Requesting Permission with *te mo ii desu ka*

（N は）V てもいいですか。

(N wa) V-te mo ii desu ka.

Is it all right if N does V?

今晩電話をしてもいいですか。

Konban denwa o shite mo ii desu ka.

Is it all right if I give you a call tonight?

This pattern is used when asking permission to do something. The subject is "I" and therefore often left unexpressed, though it may be expressed. If the subject is someone other than "I," it must be expressed or clearly understood from context. *V-te mo* literally means "if V." Aside from the translation given above ("Is it all right if N does V?"), this pattern could also be rendered as "May N do V?" For politer expressions of this sort, such as *V-sasete itadaite mo ii desu ka* and *V-sasete itadakenai deshō ka*, see my *Japanesse Verbs at a Glance*, page 52. This pattern, minus *ka*, may be used in a positive sense to give permission (*[N wa] V-te mo ii desu*; "It's all right if N does V").

Formula

(N wa) V-te mo ii desu ka.

Is it all right if N does V?

N = a noun acting as the subject of the sentence; often unexpressed

V = a verb in the *te* form indicating what action one is asking permission to take

mo = a particle meaning "if" when following a *te*-form verb in this particular pattern

入ってもいいですか。

Haitte mo ii desu ka.
May I come in?

高山：この記事をコピーしてもいいですか。

Takayama: Kono kiji o kopī shite mo ii desu ka.
May I copy this article?

桑田：いいですよ。

Kuwata: Ii desu yo.
Please do.

Note that the last sentence of this dialogue (*Ii desu yo*) essentially means *Kopī shite mo ii desu yo*, which is a positive version of the basic pattern under consideration. This is also true of the last lines in the two informal dialogues that follow.

BETWEEN MEN

高山：この記事コピーしてもいい？

Takayama: Kono kiji kopī shite mo ii?
Can I copy this article?

桑田：いいよ。

Kuwata: Ii yo.
Sure.

Basic Pattern 26   189

BETWEEN WOMEN

森：この本、借りてもいいかしら？
Mori: Kono hon, karite mo ii kashira?
Can I borrow this book?

安倍：いいわよ。
Abe: Ii wa yo.
Surely.

Variation ① Requesting Permission with *te mo kamaimasen ka*

(N は) V てもかまいませんか。
(N wa) V-te mo kamaimasen ka.
Do you mind if N does V?

明日行かなくてもかまいませんか。
Ashita ikanakute mo kamaimasen ka.
Is it all right if I don't go tomorrow?

While this variation has essentially the same meaning as Basic Pattern 26 (*[N wa] V-te mo ii desu ka*), it is somewhat politer. This difference comes from the use of the verb *kamau* ("to care about" or "to be concerned about") and the fact that it is in the negative, which seems to show consideration for the other party in anticipating the possibility of a negative answer. Literally, the pattern could be translated, "You don't mind if I V?" In the examples given here, the subject is "I" and therefore left unexpressed, though it may be expressed. If the subject is someone other than "I," it must be expressed or clearly understood from context.

(N wa) <u>V</u>-te mo kamaimasen ka.

Do you mind if N does V?

N = a noun acting as the subject of the sentence; often unexpressed

V = a verb in the *te* form indicating what action one is asking permission to take

mo = a particle meaning "if" when following a *te*-form verb in this particular pattern

kamaimasen ka = lit., "don't you mind?"; a sentence-ending verb followed by the particle *ka*, which transforms a statement into a question

Polite

乗客：ここに荷物を置いてもかまいませんか。

Jōkyaku: Koko ni nimotsu o oite mo kamaimasen ka.
Passenger: Do you mind if I leave my luggage here?

駅員：かまいませんよ。

Ekiin: Kamaimasen yo.
Station attendant: Not at all.

Informal

BETWEEN MEN

森：この本借りてもかまわない？

Mori: Kono hon karite mo kamawanai?
Mind if I borrow this book?

安倍：かまわないよ。どうぞ。

Abe: Kamawanai yo. Dōzo.
No, help yourself.

(N は) V てはいけません。

(N wa) V-te wa ikemasen.

You shouldn't do V.

鉛筆で書いてはいけません。

Enpitsu de kaite wa ikemasen.

You shouldn't write in pencil.

In this pattern for negative commands or prohibitions, a *te*-form verb is followed by *wa* and then the sentence-ending verb *ikemasen*, which basically means "shouldn't," "not proper or fitting," or "not allowed." This verb is characteristic of spoken speech rather than the written language, which perhaps accounts for its range of meanings from that which is not permitted to that which is frowned upon.

Formula

(N wa) V-te wa ikemasen.

You shouldn't do V.

N = a noun acting as the subject of the sentence; often unexpressed since it is understood to refer to the person being spoken to

V = a *te*-form verb followed by *wa*, indicating the action that is not permitted or frowned upon

ikemasen = sentence-ending verb meaning "shouldn't," "not supposed to," or "not allowed"

Polite

ここにごみを捨ててはいけません。

Koko ni gomi o sutete wa ikemasen.

You are not supposed to throw away garbage here.

部屋の中でたばこを吸ってはいけません。

Heya no naka de tabako o sutte wa ikemasen.

You shouldn't smoke in the room.

BETWEEN MEN

昇：ここでたばこ吸ってもいいかな。

Noboru: Koko de tabako sutte mo ii ka na.

Is it all right to smoke here?

孝：吸ってはいけないよ。

Takashi: Sutte wa ikenai yo.

No, it's not allowed.

Variation 1 Expressing Prohibition with *dame desu*

(N は) <u>V</u> てはだめです。

(N wa) V-te wa dame desu.

You can't do V.

早く帰ってはだめです。

Hayaku kaette wa dame desu.

You can't leave early.

This variation has essentially the same meaning as Basic Pattern 27 (*[N wa] <u>V</u>-te wa ikemasen*) in its use as a negative command or prohibition. The only difference is in the nuance of the words *dame* ("no good," "bad," "not allowed") and *ikemasen*. If a distinction were to be drawn, it might be that the former has a slightly moralistic tone while the latter is stronger in its sense of prohibition.

(N wa) <u>*V*</u>*-te wa dame desu.*

You shouldn't do V.

N = a noun acting as the subject of the sentence; often unexpressed since it is understood to refer to the person being spoken to

V = a *te*-form verb followed by *wa*, indicating the action that is not permitted

dame = a sentence-ending *na*-adjective meaning "no good," "bad," or "not allowed"

Polite

遅く来てはだめです。

Osoku kite wa dame desu.
Don't come late.

漫画ばかり読んではだめです。

Manga bakari yonde wa dame desu.
Don't be reading comics all the time.

Informal

BETWEEN WOMEN

姉：私のネックレス、使っちゃだめよ。

Ane: Watashi no nekkuresu, tsukatcha dame yo.
Older sister: You can't use my necklace.

妹：どうして、貸してよ。

Imōto: Dōshite, kashite yo.
Little sister: Why not? Just let me borrow it.

In the first sentence of this dialogue, *tsukatte wa* has become the colloquial *tsukatcha*.

CHAPTER 4

Basic Patterns 28-29

In this chapter we look at a number of patterns concerned with giving and receiving. The verbs taken up are *agemasu, moraimasu,* and *kuremasu,* both in patterns in which they take a direct object and in patterns when they are preceded by a *te*-form verb.

Basic Pattern 28 Giving with *agemasu*

<u>N1</u> は <u>N2</u> に <u>N3</u> を <u>V</u> (あげます)。
N1 wa N2 ni N3 o V (agemasu).
N1 gives N3 to N2.

私は母に、誕生日のプレゼントをあげます。
Watashi wa haha ni, tanjōbi no purezento o agemasu.
I will give a birthday present to my mother.

This pattern expresses the idea of one person giving something to someone else. The verb is the polite *agemasu* ("to give"). In this formula, N1 is the subject and is the doer or agent of the action; N2 is the indirect object of the verb or the person to which something is given. N3 is the object given. In place of *ageru*, the honorific *sashiageru* may be used when giving something to someone who is deserving of particular regard. The verb *yaru* is commonly used when giving something to animals or plants or from an adult to an child; it can also be used among family or close friends.

Formula

N1 wa N2 ni N3 o V (agemasu).

N1 gives N3 to N2.

N1 = a noun (the giver) acting as the subject of the sentence

N2 = a noun acting as the indirect object of the verb; indicating to whom something is given

N3 = a noun acting as the direct object of the verb; usually an object

V = a verb showing that something is being given; often the polite *agemasu*

Polite

私は友達に外国の切手をあげます。

Watashi wa tomodachi ni gaikoku no kitte o agemasu.

I give my friend foreign stamps.

Informal

BETWEEN WOMEN

藤原：きれいな切手ね。

Fujiwara: Kirei na kitte ne.

What beautiful stamps.

芳賀：ええ、友達にあげるの。

Haga : Ee, tomodachi ni ageru no.

Yes, I'm giving them to a friend.

In the second line of this dialogue, the direct object of the verb *ageru* has been omitted since it is understood from having appeared in the first line.

Honorific

WITH *SASHIAGERU*

その子供は女王に花をさしあげました。
Sono kodomo wa joō ni hana o sashiagemashita.
The child gave flowers to the queen.

Informal

WITH *YARU*

妻：花に水やった？
Tsuma: Hana ni mizu yatta?
Wife: Did you give water to the flowers?

夫：うん、朝やったよ。
Otto: Un, asa yatta yo.
Husband: Yes, this morning.

In the first line, the particle *o* that would ordinarily follow the direct object *mizu* has been omitted, as often happens in casual conversation.

Variation **1** Receiving with *moraimasu*

<u>N1</u> は <u>N2</u> から/に <u>N3</u> を <u>V</u>（もらいます）。
N1 wa N2 kara / ni N3 o V (moraimasu).
N1 receives N3 from N2.

私は友達からチョコレートをもらいました。
Watashi wa tomodachi kara chokorēto o moraimashita.
I received chocolate from a friend.

In contrast to Basic Pattern 28 (_N1_ wa _N2_ ni _N3_ o V [age-masu]), this variation shows receiving rather than giving. The sentence-ending verb is _moraimasu_ ("to receive"), and the subject (N1) has become the receiver. N2 (followed by _kara_ or _ni_) is the person from whom something is received, and N3 indicates what is received.

Formula

_N1_ wa _N2_ kara / ni _N3_ o _V_ (moraimasu).

N1 receives N3 from N2.

N1 = a noun (the receiver) acting as the subject of the sentence

N2 = a noun acting as the indirect object of the verb, indicating from whom something is received

N3 = a noun acting as the direct object of the verb, indicating what is given; usually an object

V = a verb showing that something is being received by the speaker or the speaker's group; often the polite _moraimasu_

Polite

五十嵐：去年のクリスマスに、お父さんから 何をもらいましたか？

Igarashi: Kyonen no kurisumasu ni, otōsan kara nani o moraimashita ka?

What did you get from your father last Christmas?

橋本：お金をもらいました。

Hashimoto: Okane o moraimashita.

I received some money.

WITH *ITADAKU*

長田：きれいな花瓶ですね。

Nagata: Kirei na kabin desu ne.

What a beautiful flower vase.

高桑：これは父が天皇陛下からいただいたんです。

Takakuwa: Kore wa chichi ga tennō-heika kara itadaita 'n desu.

My father received it from the Emperor.

Notice here that the direct object of the verb (N3; a noun indicating what has been received) has been shifted to the front of the sentence and made the topic, with the particle *o* being replaced by *wa*.

BETWEEN WOMEN

美佳：去年のクリスマスに、お父さんから何もらったの？

Mika: Kyonen no kurisumasu ni, otōsan kara nani moratta no?

What did you get from your father last Christmas?

良子：お金もらったわ。

Yoshiko: Okane moratta wa.

I received some money.

In this chacteristically informal dialogue, the particle *o*, which would normally follow *okane*, has been dropped.

<u>N1</u> は <u>N2</u> に <u>N3</u> を <u>V</u>（くれます）。

N1 wa N2 ni N3 o V (kuremasu).
N1 gives N3 to N2.

父は私にカメラをくれます。

Chichi wa watashi ni kamera o kuremasu.
My father will give me a camera.

This variation contrasts with Basic Pattern 28 (*N1 wa N2 ni N3 o V [agemasu]*) in the choice of sentence-ending verb, which is *kureru* rather than *agemasu*. Both mean "to give," but whereas *agemasu* is used from the perspective of the speaker or the speaker's group who is giving something to someone else, *kureru* is usually used from the perspective of the speaker or speaker's group who is receiving something from someone else. The honorific *kudasaru* can replace *kuremasu* when the giver is someone who deserves special respect. In this variation the subject (N1) is slightly emphasized.

Formula

N1 wa N2 ni N3 o V (kuremasu).

N1 gives N3 to N2.

N1 = a noun (the giver) acting as the subject of the sentence; not the speaker

N2 = a noun acting as the indirect object of the verb, indicating the person who is receiving something; usually the speaker or someone belonging to the speaker's group

N3 = a noun acting as the direct object of the verb, indicating what is given; usually an object

V = a verb showing that something is being given to the

speaker or someone in the speaker's group; often the polite *kuremasu*

友達がコンサートの切符をくれました。

Tomodachi ga konsāto no kippu o kuremashita.
My friend gave me a concert ticket.

Here the indirect object, indicating who is receiving the ticket and normally followed by *ni*, has been omitted since it is understood to be the speaker. This is also true of the examples that follow.

BETWEEN WOMEN

康子：友達が今晩のコンサートの切符をくれ
たの。一緒に行かない？

Yasuko: Tomodachi ga konban no konsāto no kippu o kureta no. Issho ni ikanai?
A friend gave me tickets to tonight's concert. Won't you come with me?

久子：いいわね、行くわ。

Hisako: Ii wa ne, iku wa.
That's great. I'll go.

WITH *KUDASARU*

良子：この辞書はいいですね。

Yoshiko: Kono jisho wa ii desu ne.
This dictionary is good, isn't it.

ジョン：ええ、先生がくださったんです。

Jon: Ee, sensei ga kudasatta 'n desu.
Yes, my teacher gave it to me.

N1 は N2 に N3 を V (てあげます)。

N1 wa N2 ni N3 o V (-te agemasu).

N1 does N3 for N2.

私はジョンさんに日本語を教えてあげます。

Watashi wa Jon-san ni Nihon-go o oshiete agemasu.

I teach John Japanese.

This pattern is similar to Basic Pattern 28 (*N1 wa N2 ni N3 o V [agemasu]*) in that it shows the subject giving something to another party, but it is different in that what is given is not an object but an action. The action is indicated by a *te*-form verb. Another way of expressing this is to say that the subject does something for another party as a favor. As with Basic Pattern 28, *sashiageru* can be used to show special respect, and *yaru* can be used among intimate friends or when referring to children, animals, or plants.

Formula

N1 wa N2 ni N3 o V (-te agemasu).

N1 does N3 for N2.

N1 = a noun (the giver) acting as the subject of the sentence

N2 = a noun acting as the indirect object of the verb; indicating to whom something is given

N3 = a noun acting as the direct object of the verb; usually an object

V = a *te*-form verb followed by *agemasu*, showing that something is being done for someone else

Polite

私は友達に外国の切手を送ってあげます。

Watashi wa tomodachi ni gaikoku no kitte o okutte agemasu.
I send my friend foreign stamps.

姉は弟にご飯を食べさせて上げました。

Ane wa otōto ni gohan o tabesasete agemashita.
The older sister fed her little brother.

Honorific

WITH *SASHIAGERU*

私は先生に写真を撮ってさしあげました。

Watashi wa sensei ni shashin o totte sashiagemashita.
I took pictures for my teacher.

Informal

子供：このケーキおいしいよ。

Kodomo: Kono kēki oishii yo.
Child: This cake is so good.

母：そう、また作ってあげるわ。

Haha: Sō, mata tsukutte ageru wa.
Mother: Is that so? I'll make it for you again.

In the second line, both the direct object (the cake mentioned in the first line) and the indirect object ("you," that is, the child) go unmentioned since they are understood from context.

Informal

WITH *YARU*

妻：デパートで太郎に何か買ってやった？

Tsuma: Depāto de Tarō ni nani ka katte yatta?
Wife: Did you buy Taro something at the department store?

夫：おもちゃのバスを買ってやったよ。

Otto: Omocha no basu o katte yatta yo.

Husband: I bought him a toy bus.

Variation 1   Being the Recipient of an Action with *te moraimasu*

<u>N1</u> は <u>N2</u> に/から <u>N3</u> を <u>V</u>（てもらいます）。

N1 wa N2 ni / kara N3 o V (-te moraimasu).

N1 receives N3 from N2.

林さんは友達にその本を見せてもらいます。

Hayashi-san wa tomodachi ni sono hon o misete morai-masu.

A friend will show the book to Mr. Hayashi.

This variation is similar to Basic Pattern 29 (*N1 wa N2 ni N3 o V [-te agemasu]*) and to Basic Pattern 28, Variation 1 (*N1 wa N2 kara / ni N3 o V [moraimasu]*). It is similar to the former in that a *te* form is used, and to the latter in that it employs *moraimasu*. In essence, this pattern indicates that the speaker or the speaker's group receives a favor in the form of an action from another party.

Formula

N1 wa N2 ni / kara N3 o V (-te moraimasu).

N1 receives N3 from N2.

N1 = a noun (the receiver) acting as the subject of the sentence

N2 = a noun acting as the indirect object of the verb; indicating from whom something is received

N3 = a noun acting as the direct object of the verb; usually an object

V = a *te*-form verb followed by *moraimasu*, showing that

something (an action) is being received from someone else

先生：誕生日にお父さんに何か買ってもらいましたか。

Sensei: Tanjōbi ni otōsan ni nani ka katte moraimashita ka.

Teacher: Did you get something from your father for your birthday?

学生：携帯電話を買ってもらいました。

Gakusei: Keitai-denwa o katte moraimashita.

Student: I got a cellular phone. / He bought me a cellular phone.

WITH *ITADAKU*

松原：大学でフランス語を勉強しましたか。

Matsubara: Daigaku de Furansu-go o benkyō shimashita ka.

Did you study French at college?

渡辺：はい、前田教授に教えていただきました。

Watanabe: Hai, Maeda kyōju ni oshiete itadakimashita.

Yes, I studied under Professor Maeda.

BETWEEN WOMEN

佐和子：クリスマスに、お母さんから何か買ってもらったの？

Sawako: Kurisumasu ni okāsan kara nani ka katte moratta no?

Did your mother buy you something for Christmas?

貞子：ううん、お小遣いもらったの。

Sadako: Uun, okozukai moratta no.

No, but I got some pocket money.

<u>N1</u> は <u>N2</u> に <u>N3</u> を <u>V</u>（てくれます）。

N1 wa N2 ni N3 o V (-te kuremasu).

N1 does N3 for N2.

父は私に授業料を送ってくれます。

Chichi wa watashi ni jugyō-ryō o okutte kuremasu.

My father sends me my tuition.

This variation is similar to Basic Pattern 29 (<u>*N1*</u> *wa* <u>*N2*</u> *ni* <u>*N3*</u> *o* <u>*V*</u> *[-te agemasu]*) and to Basic Pattern 28, Variation 2 (<u>*N1*</u> *wa* <u>*N2*</u> *ni* <u>*N3*</u> *o* <u>*V*</u> *[kuremasu]*). It is similar to the former in that a *te*-form is used, and to the latter in that it employs *kuremasu*. In essence, this pattern indicates that the speaker or speaker's group is receiving something from another party, who is the subject of the sentence and the giver. In contrast to Basic Pattern 28, Variation 2, the thing given is an action rather than an object alone. The honorific *kudasaru* replaces *kuremasu* when the subject of the sentence deserves special respect. In this pattern the subject (N1) is slightly emphasized.

Formula

<u>*N1*</u> *wa* <u>*N2*</u> *ni* <u>*N3*</u> *o* <u>*V*</u> *(-te kuremasu).*

N1 does N3 for N2.

N1 = a noun (the giver) acting as the subject of the sentence; not the speaker

N2 = a noun acting as the indirect object of the verb; indicating to whom something is given

N3 = a noun acting as the direct object of the verb; usually an object

V = a *te*-form verb followed by *kuremasu*, showing that something is being done for the speaker or the speaker's group

青木さんが妹に展覧会の切符を買ってくれました。

Aoki-san ga imōto ni tenran-kai no kippu o katte kuremashita.

Ms. Aoki bought my younger sister a ticket to the exhibition.

陳さんが中国料理を作ってくれました。

Chin-san ga Chūgoku-ryōri o tsukutte kuremashita.

Ms. Chin cooked Chinese food for us.

WITH *KUDASARU*

ピアノの先生が、パリでこの楽譜を買ってきてくださいました。

Piano no sensei ga, Pari de kono gakufu o katte kite kudasaimashita.

My piano teacher bought this music score for me in Paris.

BETWEEN MEN

雅彦：パソコンの使い方、どうやって覚えた？

Masahiko: Pasokon no tsukaikata, dō yatte oboeta?

How did you learn to use a personal computer?

政夫：兄が教えてくれた。

Masao: Ani ga oshiete kureta.

My big brother taught me.

Basic Patterns 30-41

CHAPTER 5

This chapter deals with patterns that help you express what you would like or plan to do, what you have the ability to do, and what you have experienced.

Basic Pattern 30 Inviting with *V-masen ka*

(N は) V ません か。
(N wa) V-masen ka.
Won't you do V (with me)?

映画を見に行きませんか。
Eiga o mi ni ikimasen ka.
Won't you go to see a movie with me?

This pattern provides a way of inviting someone to do something. That something is indicated by the verb, which is in the negative form (*masen*) of a *masu* verb. The verb is followed by a sentence-ending *ka*, which turns what would otherwise be a statement into a question. The verb is in the negative form since that form seems to show more consideration for the other party, who may in fact wish to give a negative answer. The subject of the sentence is the person who is being invited, and since this is generally clear from context, it is usually omitted.

Formula

(N wa) V-masen ka.

Won't you do V (with me)?

N = a noun acting as the subject of the sentence; here, the person being invited and usually not expressed

V = a verb in the negative form followed by a question-forming *ka*

Polite

田久保：お茶を飲みに行きませんか。

Takubo: Ocha o nomi ni ikimasen ka.

Shall we go out for a cup of tea?

島本：いいですね。行きましょう。

Shimamoto: Ii desu ne. Ikimashō.

That's a good idea. Let's go.

Informal

BETWEEN WOMEN

頼子：明日泳ぎに行かない？

Yoriko: Ashita oyogi ni ikanai?

How about going swimming tomorrow?

美加：行く、行く。

Mika: Iku, iku.

Great. I'll go, I'll go.

Notice in the question part of this dialogue that the sentence-ending *ka* has been omitted, which is typical of informal conversation.

V ましょう。

V-mashō.

Let's do V.

飲みましょう。

Nomimashō.

Let's drink.

This pattern provides a way of inviting someone to do something that is a little more direct than that given in Basic Pattern 30 (*[N wa] V-masen ka*). This directness comes from the fact that the verb is in a positive, not negative, form and that it is not a question. An invitation of this sort is most likely to be made when it seems that the other party is very likely to accept.

Formula

V-mashō.

Let's do V.

V = a verb in the *mashō* form ("let's V") indicating what one is inviting the other party to do

Polite

横田：五時ですから、帰りましょう。

Yokota: Go-ji desu kara, kaerimashō.

It is 5:00, so let's leave.

山村：そうしましょう。

Yamamura: Sō shimashō.

Let's do that.

亮：もう5時だから帰ろう。

Tōru: Mō go-ji da kara kaerō.

It is already five. Let's go home.

孝夫：うん、そうしよう。

Takao: Un, sō shiyō.

Yeah, let's get going.

For more information about verb conjugations, see my *Japanese Verbs at a Glance*.

Variation ① Inviting with *V-mashō ka*

V̲ましょうか。   **飲みましょうか。**

V-mashō ka.   *Nomimashō ka.*

Shall we do V?   Shall we drink?

In this variation on Basic Pattern 31 (V̲-*mashō*), *ka* has been added to the end of the sentence, turning what was a direct statement into a question. Because of this, the inviation to do something becomes more of a suggestion.

V̲-*mashō ka.*

Shall we do V?

V = a verb in the *mashō* form ("let's V") that indicates what one is inviting the other party to do; followed by question-forming *ka* at the end of the sentence

富田：まだ時間がありますから、映画を見ま
しょうか。

Tomita: Mada jikan ga arimasu kara, eiga o mimashō ka.

We still have time, so why don't we see a movie?

小川：そうしましょう。

Ogawa: Sō shimashō.

Let's do that.

Basic Pattern 32 Showing Intention with *tsumori*

N は **V** つもりです。

N wa V tsumori desu.

N intends to do V.

私はフランスへ行くつもりです。

Watashi wa Furansu e iku tsumori desu.

I plan to go to France.

This pattern provides a way of saying what one plans or intends to do. The main feature is the noun *tsumori*, whose meaning here is "plan" or "intention." It can be modified by a plain-form verb or by *sono, ano,* etc.

Formula

_N_ wa _V_ tsumori desu.

N intends to do V.

N = a noun acting as the subject of the sentence; can refer to the speaker or to someone else

V = a verb in plain form, followed by *tsumori desu*

桑野：もう音楽史の本を読みましたか。

Kuwano: Mō ongaku-shi no hon o yomimashita ka.

Have you read the book on the history of music yet?

野島：いいえ、明日図書館でその本を借りる
つもりです。

Nojima: Iie, ashita tosho-kan de sono hon o kariru tsumori desu.

No, I intend to borrow the book from the library tomorrow.

BETWEEN WOMEN

宏美：夏休み、旅行へ行く？

Hiromi: Natsu-yasumi, ryokō e iku?

Are you going somewhere during summer vacation?

由佳：行くわ、今年はスイスへ行くつもり。

Yuka: Iku wa, kotoshi wa Suisu e iku tsumori.

Yes, I am. I plan to go to Switzerland this year.

宏美：スイスへ？いいなあ！

Hiromi: Suisu e? Ii naa!

To Switzerland? How nice!

Variation 1 Showing Negative Intention with *V-nai tsumori*

N は V ないつもりです。

N wa V-nai tsumori desu.

N intends not to do V.

私はその映画を見ないつもりです。

Watashi wa sono eiga o minai tsumori desu.

I plan not to see that movie. / I don't plan to see that movie.

In this variation on Basic Pattern 32 (<u>N</u> wa <u>V</u> tsumori desu), the plain-form verb preceding tsumori takes a negative form, indicating what one plans not to do.

Formula

<u>N</u> wa <u>V</u>-nai tsumori desu.

N intends not to do V.

N = a noun acting as the subject of the sentence; can refer to the speaker or to someone else

V = a verb in a negative plain form, followed by *tsumori desu*

Polite

叔父：受験勉強大変でしょう？

Oji: Juken-benkyō taihen deshō?

Uncle: You must be studying hard for the college exams.

甥：僕、大学へ行かないつもりです。

Oi: Boku, daigaku e ikanai tsumori desu.

Nephew: I don't plan to go to college.

Informal

BETWEEN MEN

迫田：飲みに行かない？

Sakota: Nomi ni ikanai?

Want to go for a drink?

野添：いや、明日の朝5時にゴルフに行くから、今晩は飲まないつもり。

Nozoe: Iya, ashita no asa go-ji ni gorufu ni iku kara, konban wa nomanai tsumori.

No, I'm going to play golf tomorrow morning at five, so I don't plan to drink tonight.

One's intention of not doing something can also be conveyed by attaching the polite *dewa arimasen* or the slightly more emphatic and colloquial *ja arimasen* to *tsumori*.

私はそのプロジェクトに参加するつもりじゃありません。

Watashi wa sono purojekuto ni sanka suru tsumori ja arimasen.

I have no intention of joining that project.

Basic Pattern **33** Showing Intention with *V-yō to omoimasu*

N は V よう(おう)と思います。

N wa V-yō (ō) to omoimasu.

N is thinking of doing V.

私は大学で法律を勉強しようと思います。

Watashi wa daigaku de hōritsu o benkyō shiyō to omoimasu.

I am thinking of studying law at college.

This pattern is similar to Basic Pattern 32 (*N wa V tsumori desu*) in that it conveys intention, but it is different in that the intention is less decisive. In this pattern, the subject of the sentence is taking some action under consideration, not having fully decided yet. This is accomplished by the volitional form (*V-yō [ō]*) plus *to omoimasu* or *to omotte imasu*. With the former, the subject must be the speaker, but with the latter it may be the speaker or another party. For information about the volitional form, see my *Japanese Verbs at a Glance*.

<u>N</u> wa <u>V</u>-yō (ō) to omoimasu.

N is thinking of doing V.

N = a noun acting as the subject of the sentence; with *to omoimasu*, the subject must be the speaker, but with *to omotte imasu* it may be the speaker or someone else

V = a verb in the volitional form (*V-yō [ō]*) followed by *to omoimasu* or *to omotte imasu*.

Polite

今晩は外で食事をしようと思います。

Konban wa soto de shokuji o shiyō to omoimasu.

Tonight I'm thinking of eating out.

私は来年の夏からアメリカの大学で勉強しようと思っています。

Watashi wa rainen no natsu kara Amerika no daigaku de benkyō shiyō to omotte imasu.

I am thinking of studying at an America college from next summer.

Informal

BETWEEN MEN

洋：大学を卒業したら、どんな会社に勤めるつもり？

Hiroshi: Daigaku o sotsugyō shitara, donna kaisha ni tsutomeru tsumori?

What kind of company do you plan to work for after you graduate from college?

孝夫：卒業したら、大学院に行こうと思ってる。

Takao: Sotsugyō shitara, daigaku-in ni ikō to omotte 'ru.

After graduation I'm thinking of going to graduate school.

BETWEEN WOMEN

圭子：日曜日、何するつもり？

Keiko: Nichiyōbi, nani suru tsumori?

What are you planning to do on Sunday?

恵：歌舞伎見ようと思ってるの。

Megumi: Kabuki miyō to omotte 'ru no.

I'm thinking of seeing Kabuki.

In place of *omotte imasu*, it is possible to use *kangaete imasu*. However, *omoimasu* cannot be replaced by *kangaemasu*.

来週から毎日30分ジョギングをしようと考えています。

Raishū kara mainichi sanjuppun jogingu o shiyō to kangaete imasu.

I'm thinking of jogging for half an hour a day starting next week.

Basic Pattern 34 Expressing a Desire with *V-tai*

<u>N</u> は <u>V</u> たいです。

N wa V-tai desu.

N wants to do V.

私は新しい車が買いたいです。

Watashi wa atarashii kuruma ga kaitai desu.

I want to buy a new car.

This pattern describes a speaker's wish or desire by attaching the auxiliary verb *tai* ("want to") to a *masu* stem (a *masu*-form verb after *masu* has been removed). The *masu* stem says what the speaker wants to do. If the subject is someone other than the speaker, *tai* is replaced by the verb *tagarimasu* ("want to").

<u>*N*</u> *wa* <u>*V*</u>*-tai desu.*

N wants to do V.

N= a noun acting as the subject of the sentence

V = a verb in the *masu*-stem form to which *tai* ("want to") is attached when the speaker is the subject, and *tagaru* ("want to") attached when the speaker is not the subject

武田：もうすぐお正月ですね。どこかへ行きますか。

Takeda: Mō sugu oshōgatsu desu ne. Doko ka e ikimasu ka.

New Year's is almost here. Are you going somewhere?

中川：お正月休みにはスイスへスキーに行きたいです。

Nakagawa: Oshōgatsu-yasumi ni wa Suisu e skī ni ikitai desu.

For New Year's vacation I want to go to Switzerland and ski.

BETWEEN MEN

健一：休みにどこへ行きたい？

Kenichi: Yasumi ni doko e ikitai?

Where do you want to go during the vacation?

武：バリ島なんかへ行ってみたい。

Takeshi: Bari-tō nanka e itte mitai.

I want to go someplace like Bali.

When talking about a another party, *V-tagarimasu* or *V-tagatte imasu* are used.

子供はファミコンをしたがります。

Kodomo wa famikon o shitagarimasu.

Children want / like to play computer games.

妹はピアノを買いたがっています。

Imōto wa piano o kaitagatte imasu.

My younger sister wants to buy a piano.

Variation ❶ Expressing a Desire with *V-tai to omoimasu*

<u>N</u> は <u>V</u> たいと思います／思っています。

N wa V-tai to omoimasu / omotte imasu.

N would like to do V.

私は来週休みをとりたいと思います。

Watashi wa raishū yasumi o toritai to omoimasu.

I would like to take next week off. / I'm thinking of taking next week off.

This variation is similar to Basic Pattern 34 (<u>N</u> *wa* <u>V</u>-*tai desu*) in its use of *tai* ("want to") and in its indication of what the subject wants to do. Through the addition of *omoimasu*, however, the expression of personal desire is somewhat softened. If the speaker is the subject of the sentence, the sentence-ending verb can be either *omoimasu* or *omotte imasu*, but if someone else is the subject, the verb must be *omotte imasu*.

<u>N</u> wa <u>V</u>-tai to omoimasu / omotte imasu.

N would like to do V.

N = a noun acting as the subject of the sentence

V = a verb in the *masu*-stem form plus *tai* ("want to")
followed by *to omoimasu* or *to omotte imasu*

私は来年新しい仕事を始めたいと思っています。

Watashi wa rainen atarashii shigoto o hajimetai to omotte imasu.

I'd like to start a new business next year. / I'm thinking
of starting a new business next year.

斉藤：園田さんのあさってのご予定は？

Saitō: Sonoda-san no asatte no goyotei wa?

How's your schedule for the day after tomorrow?

園田：田中商事の部長に会って、新しいプロジェクトの相談をしたいと思っています。

Sonoda: Tanaka Shōji no buchō ni atte, atarashii puro-jekuto no sōdan o shitai to omotte imasu.

I'm thinking of meeting the department director at Tanaka
Trading Company and talking over a new project.

Basic Pattern ⟨35⟩ Expressing Ability with *V koto ga dekimasu*

<u>N</u> は <u>V</u> ことができます。

N wa V koto ga dekimasu.

N can do V.

私は車を運転することができます。

Watashi wa kuruma o unten suru koto ga dekimasu.

I can drive a car.

This pattern provides a means of expressing whether or not one has the ability to do some action or whether circumstances permit a certain action. It consists of *koto ga dekimasu* ("a thing can be done"), in which *koto* is the subject of the verb *dekiru*, and the plain-form verb that precedes *koto* indicates the action that can be done. This pattern can be transformed into a negative statement by replacing *dekimasu* with *dekimasen* (informally, *dekimasen* becomes *dekinai*).

Formula

N wa V koto ga dekimasu.

N can do V.

N = a noun acting as the topic of the sentence (*koto* is the subject)

V = a verb in plain form followed by *koto ga dekimasu*

Polite

富田：岡さんはフランス語を話すことができますか。

Tomita: Oka-san wa Furansu-go o hanasu koto ga dekimasu ka.

Can Mr. Oka speak French?

林：できますよ。フランスの大学を卒業していますから。

Hayashi: Dekimasu yo. Furansu no daigaku o sotsugyō shite imasu kara.

Yes, he can. He graduated from a French university.

Informal

BETWEEN WOMEN

早苗：今からでも新幹線の切符、買うことできる？

Sanae: Ima kara demo shinkan-sen no kippu, kau koto dekiru?
Is it possible to get Shinkansen tickets even now?

時子：出来ると思うけど。

Tokiko: Dekiru to omou kedo.

I think so.

Basic Pattern **36** **Expressing Ability with** *V(potential)-masu*

N は V (potential)ます。

N wa V(potential)-masu.

N can do V.

私は今晩早く帰れます。

Watashi wa konban hayaku kaeremasu.

I can go home early tonight.

This pattern is similar to Basic Pattern 35 (<u>N</u> *wa* <u>V</u> *koto ga dekimasu*) in that it shows what can be done or is possible to do. It is different in that it uses the potential form of the verb (see my *Japanese Verbs at a Glance* for more information on potential verbs) rather than *koto ga dekimasu.*

Formula

<u>N</u> wa <u>V</u>(potential)-masu.

N can do V.

N = a noun acting as the subject of the sentence

V = a verb in potential form plus *masu*

Polite

小川：課長は飲めますか。

Ogawa: Kachō wa nomemasu ka.

Can the section manager drink?

野添：部長はかなり強いんですが、課長は飲めないようですよ。

Nozoe: Buchō wa kanari tsuyoi 'n desu ga, kachō wa nomenai yō desu yo.

The department director is a good drinker, but apparently the section manager isn't.

Informal

BETWEEN MEN

鈴木：橋本君は泳ぎはうまいの？

Suzuki: Hashimoto-kun wa oyogi wa umai no?

Are you a good swimmer, Hashimoto?

橋本：子供の時北海道に住んでいたんで、全然泳げないんだよ。でもスキーはできるよ。

Hashimoto: Kodomo no toki Hokkaidō ni sunde ita 'n de, zenzen oyogenai 'n da yo. Demo skī wa dekiru yo.

I lived in (snow-bound) Hokkaido when I was small, so I can't swim at all. But I can ski.

Basic Pattern **37** Becoming Able with *V(potential) yō ni narimasu*

<u>N1</u> は <u>N2</u> が <u>V</u>(potential)ようになります／なりました。

N1 wa N2 ga V (potential) yō ni narimasu / narimashita.

N1 becomes / became able to V N2.

私はショパンのワルツが弾けるようになりました。

Watashi wa Shopan no warutsu ga hikeru yō ni nari-mashita.

I became able to play Chopin's waltzes.

This pattern indicates that one will soon reach, or has reached, a stage at which what was impossible before is now possible. That which can now be done is represented by a verb in the plain potential form. The fact that one will soon be able to do it is indicated by *yō ni narimasu*, and that one has now reached the point of being able to do it by *yō ni narimashita*. Note that N1 is the topic of the sentence while N2 is the subject. Either can be omitted if understood from the flow of the conversation or if unnecessary to the meaning.

N1 wa N2 ga V (potential) yō ni narimasu / narimashita.

N1 becomes / became able to V N2.

N1 = a noun acting as the topic of the sentence

N2 = a noun acting as the subject of the sentence

V = a verb in potential form plus *yō ni narimasu / narimashita*

須藤：この頃英語の勉強はどうですか。

Sudo: Konogoro Eigo no benkyō wa dō desu ka.

How are your English studies going these days?

五十嵐：やっと英字新聞が読めるようになりましたよ。

Igarashi: Yatto Eiji-shinbun ga yomeru yō ni narimashita yo.

I have finally gotten so I can read English newspapers.

BETWEEN WOMEN

高山：お宅の赤ちゃん、大きくなったでしょう？

Takayama: Otaku no akachan, ōkiku natta deshō?

Your baby must be quite big by now.

斉藤：先週から歩けるようになったのよ。

Saitō: Senshū kara arukeru yō ni natta no yo.

She started walking last week.

Variation 1 Commencing an Action with *V yō ni narimasu*

<u>N</u>は<u>V</u>ようになります/なりました。

N wa V yō ni narimasu / narimashita.

N starts / started to do V.

隣の子供はこの春から、幼稚園へ行くように なりました。

Tonari no kodomo wa kono haru kara, yōchien e iku yō ni narimashita.

Our neighbor's child started going to kindergarten this spring.

This variation differs from Basic Pattern 37 (<u>N1</u> wa <u>N2</u> ga <u>V</u> (*potential*) *yō ni narimasu / narimashita*) in that the verb preceding *yō* is in the plain rather than the potential form. This replacement results in a change of meaning from "becoming able to do something" to "becoming (or starting) to do something." In this variation, as in the Basic Pattern, there is usually reference to a point in time when the change took place, either implicit or explicit.

Formula

<u>N</u> wa <u>V</u> yō ni narimasu / narimashita.

N starts / started to do V.

N = a noun acting as the subject of the sentence

V = a verb in plain form followed by *yō ni narimasu / narimashita*

杉田：この頃ジョンさんは、お寿司を食べる
　　　ようになりましたね。

Sugita: Konogoro Jon-san wa, osushi o taberu yō ni nari-
mashita ne.

John, I see you have started eating sushi these days.

ジョン：はい、刺身もよく食べるようになり
　　　ました。

Jon: Hai, sashimi mo yoku taberu yō ni narimashita.

That's right. I have started eating sashimi a lot, too.

BETWEEN WOMEN

芦田：この頃幸恵ちゃん、お元気？

Ashida: Konogoro Yukie-chan, ogenki?

How is little Yukie these days?

戸川：ええ、お陰様で。中学生になったら、
　　　やっと勉強するようになったわ。

Togawa: Ee, okage-sama de. Chūgaku-sei ni nattara,
yatto benkyō suru yō ni natta wa.

Thank you for asking. After becoming a junior high
student, she has finally started studying.

Variation **2** Avoiding an Action with *V-nai yō ni V-masu*

<u>N</u> は <u>V1</u> ないように <u>V2</u> ます。

N wa V1-nai yō ni V2-masu.

N does V2 in order not to do V1.

私は風邪を引かないように毎晩早く寝ます。

Watashi wa kaze o hikanai yō ni maiban hayaku nemasu.

I go to bed early every night so that I don't catch a cold.

This variation shares with Basic Pattern 37 (<u>N1</u> wa <u>N2</u> ga <u>V</u> [potential] yō ni narimasu / narimashita) the use of yō ni ("so that"), which has the function of connecting the negative plain-form verb that precedes it and the sentence-ending verb that follows. Here, yō ni might be better translated as "in order to": the subject does one action *in order to* avoid another.

Formula

<u>N</u> wa <u>V1-nai yō ni</u> <u>V2-masu.</u>
N does V2 in order not to do V1.
N = a noun acting as the subject the sentence
V1 = a verb in plain negative form plus yō ni V-masu

Polite

松田：それは何ですか。
Matsuda: Sore wa nan desu ka.
What's that?

杉山：中国語の単語のカードです。忘れないように覚えた言葉をカードに書いてあるんです。
Sugiyama: Chūgoku-go no tango no kādo desu. Wasure-nai yō ni oboeta kotoba o kādo ni kaite aru 'n desu.
These are Chinese vocabulary cards. I have written on them the words I've learned so as not to forget them.

Informal

BETWEEN MEN

吉川：もう昼食終わった？
Yoshikawa: Mō chūshoku owatta?
Have you eaten lunch?

内海：まだだよ。
Utsumi: Mada da yo.
Not yet.

吉川：会議に遅れないように、早く食べてきて。

Yoshikawa: Kaigi ni okurenai yō ni, hayaku tabete kite.

Go and get a quick bite to eat so you're not late for the meeting.

Basic Pattern **38** Stating Previous Experience (*V-ta koto ga arimasu*)

<u>N</u> は<u>V</u>たことがあります。

N wa V-ta koto ga arimasu.

N has had the experience of doing V.

私はラスベガスへ行ったことがあります。

Watashi wa Rasubegasu e itta koto ga arimasu.

I have been to Las Vegas.

This pattern is used to indicate that one has had the experience of doing something, and that something is expressed by a verb in plain-form past tense before *koto ga arimasu* ("to have the experience").

Formula

<u>N</u> wa <u>V</u>-ta koto ga arimasu.

N has had the experience of doing V.

N = a noun acting as the subject of the sentence

V = a verb in plain past form followed by *koto ga arimasu*

Polite

吉田：あの会社の社長に会った事がありますか。

Yoshida: Ano kaisha no shachō ni atta koto ga arimasu ka.

Have you ever met the president of that company?

笠原：ええ、先月ゴルフ場で会いました。い
　　　い人でしたよ。吉田さんは？

*Kasahara: Ee, sengetsu gorufu-jō de aimashita. Ii hito
deshita yo. Yoshida-san wa?*

Yes, I met him on the golf course last month. He's a
nice man. How about you?

吉田：私はまだ一度も会ったことがないんです。

Yoshida: Watashi wa mada ichido mo atta koto ga nai 'n desu.

I've never met him.

Note that *ichido mo* ("even once") reinforces the negative
meaning.

Informal

BETWEEN WOMEN

園子：インドの映画見たことある？

Sonoko: Indo no eiga mita koto aru?

Have you ever seen an Indian movie?

宏美：ないわ。見たことあるの？

Hiromi: Nai wa. Mita koto aru no?

No. Have you?

Basic Pattern **39** Indicating Habitual Action (*V koto ga/mo arimasu*)

Nは**V**ことが／も　あります。

N wa V koto ga / mo arimasu.

N occasionally does V.

私は友達とコンサートに行くことがあります。

Watashi wa tomodachi to konsāto ni iku koto ga arimasu.

I occasionally go to concerts with friends.

This pattern indicates that the subject of the sentence occasionally takes a certain action over a period of time. It is formed by a plain-form verb in the present tense followed by *koto ga arimasu* ("to have the experience of"). The particle *mo* often replaces *ga*.

Formula

<u>N</u> wa <u>V</u> koto ga / mo arimasu.

N occasionally does V.

N = a noun acting as the subject

V = a plain-form verb in the present tense followed by *koto ga / mo arimasu*

Polite

小松：土曜日は何をしていますか。

Komatsu: Doyōbi wa nani o shite imasu ka.

How do you spend Saturdays?

広津：そうですね。ゴルフに行くこともありますし、家でのんびりすることもありますよ。

Hirotsu: Sō desu ne. Gorufu ni iku koto mo arimasu shi, uchi de nonbiri suru koto mo arimasu yo.

Well, sometimes I go golfing and sometimes I stay at home and relax.

Informal

BETWEEN WOMEN

ゆき：この頃、飲みに行くことある？

Yuki: Konogoro, nomi ni iku koto aru?

Do you ever go out drinking these days?

信子：あまり行かない。でも晩御飯食べに行くことあるわよ。

Nobuko: Amari ikanai. Demo ban-gohan tabe ni iku koto aru wa yo.

Not very often. But sometimes I do go out for dinner.

A similar pattern in form and somewhat similar in meaning is that made up of a plain-form verb in the present tense plus *koto ni suru*, meaning "to make it a rule or a habit to do V."

私は毎朝 6 時に起きることにしています。

Watashi wa maiasa roku-ji ni okiru koto ni shite imasu.

I make it a rule to get up at 6:00 every morning.

Variation 1 **Indicating Habitual Actions (*V-tari V-tari shimasu*)**

<u>N</u> は <u>V1</u> たり <u>V2</u> たりします。

N wa V1-tari V2-tari shimasu.

Sometimes N does V1 or V2 or the like.

私は夜、テレビを見たり、本を読んだりします。

Watashi wa yoru, terebi o mitari, hon o yondari shimasu.

At night I sometimes watch TV, read books, or something like that.

This pattern is a variation of Basic Pattern 39 (<u>N</u> *wa* <u>V</u> *koto ga / mo arimasu*) in that it has reference to actions that have occurred in the past. It is different in that a number of actions are involved; they occur in no specific order; they do not necessarily occur in a set interval of time; and they hint that other actions of a similar type could be added to the list. The verbs indicating the actions are in the past tense (-*ta* form) with -*ri* attached, and they are followed by *shimasu* (or *shimashita* when referring to what one did in the past).

Formula

N wa *V1*-tari *V2*-tari shimasu.
Sometimes N does V1 or V2 or the like.
N = a noun acting as the subject of the sentence
V1= a verb in the *tari* form
V2= a verb in the *tari* form followed by *shimasu*

Polite

高山：冬はどんなスポーツをなさるんですか。
Takayama: Fuyu wa donna spōtsu o nasaru 'n desu ka.
What kind of sports do you do during the winter?

園田：私はスキーをしたり、スケートをしたりします。
Sonoda: Watashi wa sukī o shitari, sukēto o shitari shimasu.
I ski, ice-skate, and so on.

Informal

BETWEEN WOMEN

良子：この頃週末は何してるの？
Yoshiko: Konogoro shūmatsu wa nani shite 'ru no?
What do you do on weekends these days?

さおり：そうね、映画に行ったり、買い物に行ったりしてるわ。
Saori: Sō ne, eiga ni ittari, kaimono ni ittari shite 'ru wa.
Well, I go to see movies or go shopping, and stuff like that.

<u>N</u> は <u>V</u> たほうがいい / よかったです。

N wa V-ta hō ga ii / yokatta desu.
You should do / should have done V.

その本は読んだほうがいい / よかったですよ。

Sono hon wa yonda hō ga ii / yokatta desu yo.
You should read / should have read that book.

This pattern shows how to give advice, make a suggestion, or even express a wish that one had taken a certain course of action, referring to future or past events. This is done with the phrase *hō ga ii / yokatta* preceded by a verb in the plain past tense. *Hō ga ii / yokatta* literally means "alternative is / was good." The alternative being suggested is obviously the one expressed by this phrase, but the other alternative often remains unspoken. The unspoken alternative is often simply taking no action at all; e.g., in the example above, reading the book is better than not reading it. The subject of this pattern is *hō* (marked by *ga*), and the topic is the person to whom the advice is being directed (marked by *wa*); since this person is often "you" or "I," it is frequently omitted as being understood from context.

Formula

<u>N</u> wa <u>V</u>-ta hō ga ii / yokatta desu.
You should do / should have done V.
N = a noun acting as the topic of the sentence
V = a verb in plain past form followed by *hō ga ii / yokatta desu*

小田：どうしましたか。

Oda: Dō shimashita ka.

What's wrong?

福原：頭が痛いんです。

Fukuhara: Atama ga itai 'n desu.

I have a headache.

小田：それはいけませんね。早く帰って寝た
ほうがいいですよ。

*Oda: Sore wa ikemasen ne. Hayaku kaette neta hō ga ii
desu yo.*

That's too bad. You ought to go home early and lie down.

BETWEEN MEN

崎山：台風が来そうだけど、明日のゴルフ、
どうする？

Sakiyama: Taifū ga kisō da kedo, ashita no gorufu, dō suru?

It looks like a typhoon's coming. What'll we do about
tomorrow's golf?

三浦：やめたほうがいいね。

Miura: Yameta hō ga ii ne.

We'd better call it off.

Variation **1** Offering Advice with *V-nai hō ga ii/yokatta*

<u>N</u>は<u>V</u>ないほうがいい / よかったです。

N wa V-nai hō ga ii / yokatta desu.

You shouldn't do / shouldn't have done V.

あのレストランへ行かないほうがいい／よかったですよ。

Ano resutoran e ikanai hō ga ii / yokatta desu yo.

You shouldn't go / shouldn't have gone to that restaurant.

While Basic Pattern 40 (*N wa V-ta hō ga ii / yokatta desu*) suggests that a certain action be taken, this variation suggests that it not be taken. This is accomplished by putting the verb that precedes *hō* in the plain-past negative form. As with the basic pattern, the subject of this variation is *hō* (marked by *ga*), and the topic (marked by *wa*) is the person to whom the advice is being directed; since this person is often "you" or "I," it is omitted as being understood from context.

Formula

N wa V-nai hō ga ii / yokatta desu.

You shouldn't do / shouldn't have done V.

N = a noun acting as the topic of the sentence

V = a verb in plain-past negative form preceding *hō ga ii / yokatta desu*

Polite

古賀：タクシーで行きましょうか。

Koga: Takushī de ikimashō ka.

Shall we go by taxi?

大竹：いや、今道が込んでいますから、タクシーで行かないほうがいいですよ。

Ōtake: Iya, ima michi ga konde imasu kara, takushī de ikanai hō ga ii desu yo.

No, the roads are crowded now, so we had better not go by taxi.

神谷：雨が降ってきましたね。

Kamiya: Ame ga futte kimashita ne.

It has started to rain, hasn't it.

下村：ええ、今日は山へ来ないほうが良かったですね。

Shimomura: Ee, kyō wa yama e konai hō ga yokatta desu ne.

Yes. Maybe we shouldn't have come up to the mountains today.

Informal

BETWEEN YOUNG MEN

大沼：危ないから、そんなにスピード出さないほうがいいよ。

Ōnuma: Abunai kara, sonna ni supīdo dasanai hō ga ii yo.

You shouldn't drive so fast. It's dangerous.

緒方：大丈夫だよ、この道慣れてるんだから。

Ogata: Daijōbu da yo, kono michi narete 'ru 'n da kara.

Don't worry. I'm familiar with this road.

Informal

BETWEEN GIRLS

ゆり子：そのスカート、ちょっと短かったね。

Yuriko: Sono sukāto, chotto mijikakatta ne.

That skirt seems to be a bit short.

美加：そう、これ買わないほうが良かったわ。

Mika: Sō, kore kawanai hō ga yokatta wa.

You're right. I shouldn't have bought it.

<u>N</u> は <u>V</u> ておきます。

N wa V-te okimasu.

N does V beforehand.

ビールを冷やしておきます。

Bīru o hiyashite okimasu.

I'll go ahead and cool the beer.

This pattern provides a means of saying that a certain action (*te*-form verb) is done in preparation for a upcoming event: e.g., putting the beer in the refrigerator in preparation for a party, or putting the papers for a meeting on the director's desk so that he can go over them prior to the meeting. "To do something beforehand" is represented by *okimasu*, which also appears in its past-tense form as *okimashita*.

Formula

<u>N</u> *wa* <u>V</u>-te okimasu.

N does V beforehand.

N = a noun acting as the subject of the sentence

V = a verb in *te* form followed by *okimasu*

Polite

部長：会議の書類はどこですか。

Buchō: Kaigi no shorui wa doko desu ka.

Department director: Where are the papers for the meeting?

川口：机の上に置いておきました。

Kawaguchi: Tsukue no ue ni oite okimashita.

I put them on your desk, ready for you.

BETWEEN MOTHER AND DAUGHTER

母親：来週京都へ行くんでしょう。新幹線の切符、買っておいたほうがいいわよ。

Hahaoya: Raishū Kyōto e iku 'n deshō. Shinkan-sen no kippu, katte oita hō ga ii wa yo.

Mother: You're going to Kyōto next week, right? You ought to get your Shinkansen ticket beforehand.

娘：買ったわよ。それにホテルも予約しておいたわ。

Musume: Katta wa yo. Sore ni hoteru mo yoyaku shite oita wa.

Daughter: I did. And I already made hotel reservations too.

Basic Patterns 42-46

This chapter begins with somewhat complicated verb conjugations in patterns expressing obligation, duty, or necessity—or the lack thereof. It moves on to modification of the noun, which always presents a problem since this modification precedes the noun rather than follows it, as is the case in English. The concluding patterns and variations present different ways of expressing hearsay knowledge, supposition, and conjecture.

Basic Pattern 42 Duty/Necessity (*V-nakereba narimasen/ikemasen*)

<u>N</u>は<u>V</u>なければなりません／いけません。

N wa V-nakereba narimasen / ikemasen.
N must do V.

私は5時までに、家に帰らなければなりません。

Watashi wa go-ji made ni, ie ni kaeranakereba narimasen.
I have to go home by five.

This pattern expresses what one must do out of duty, obligation, or some other type of necessity. It involves replacing *nai* in the plain negative form of a verb with *nakereba* (e.g., the plain negative form of *taberu* is *tabenai*, which becomes *tabenakereba*). This form means "if one does not do V," and it is followed by *narimasen* ("won't do") or *ikemasen* ("is no good"). Thus *tabenakereba narimasen / ikemasen* means "one must eat." In the spoken language, *nakucha* or *nakerya* often replace *nakereba*.

Formula

N wa V-nakereba narimasen / ikemasen.
N must do V.
N = a noun acting as the subject of the sentence
V = a verb in the *nakereba* form followed by *narimasen / ikemasen*

Polite

岸：今日は残業をしなければなりません。
Kishi: Kyō wa zangyō o shinakereba narimasen.
I have to do overtime today.

川口：ずいぶん忙しいんですね。
Kawaguchi: Zuibun isogashii 'n desu ne.
You're very busy, aren't you.

Informal

BETWEEN WOMEN

片岡：今晩映画見に行かない？
Kataoka: Konban eiga mi ni ikanai?
Want to go and see a movie tonight?

小出：今晩はだめ。早く帰らなくちゃならないの。

Koide: Konban wa dame. Hayaku kaeranakucha naranai no.
Tonight's no good. I've got to get home early.

<u>N</u>は<u>V</u>なくてもいいです / かまいません。

N wa V-nakute mo ii desu / kamaimasen.
N doesn't have to do V.

宿題は明日までにしなくてもいいです。

Shukudai wa ashita made ni shinakute mo ii desu.
You don't have to finish your homework by tomorrow.

This pattern presents the reverse of Basic Pattern 42 (<u>N</u> *wa* <u>V</u>*-nakereba narimasen / ikemasen*), which expresses what must be done. Here, it is what need not be done that is the point of the pattern. *Nakute* is added to the *nai* stem of a verb and followed by *mo* ("even"), producing "even if you don't V." With the addition of the sentence-ending *ii desu* or *kamaimasen* ("it doesn't matter"), the result is "even if you don't V, it's all right": that is, "you don't have to do V."

<u>N</u> *wa* <u>V</u>*-nakute mo ii desu / kamaimasen.*

N doesn't have to do V.

N = a noun acting as the subject of the sentence

V = a *nai*-stem verb followed by *nakute mo ii desu / kamaimasen*

学生：明日も実験をしなければいけませんか。

Gakusei: Ashita mo jikken o shinakereba ikemasen ka.

Student: Do we have to do an experiment tomorrow too?

教授：いや、明日は土曜日だからしなくても
いいですよ。

Kyōju: Iya, ashita wa doyōbi da kara shinakute mo ii desu yo.

Professor: No, since tomorrow's Saturday, you don't
have to.

Basic Pattern 44 Verb Modifying Noun (*V N*)

N1 は **V N2** です。

N1 wa V N2 desu.

N1 is N2 who does V.

伊東さんは今年卒業する学生です。

Itō-san wa kotoshi sotsugyō suru gakusei desu.

Mr. Ito is a student who is graduating this year.

This pattern shows that a verb in the plain present, plain
past, or plain present progressive (*-te iru*) tenses can be
placed before a noun to modify it. The verb itself can
have a direct or indirect object, creating quite a complex
modifier. Since the verb precedes the noun rather than
follows it, this *N1 wa V N2 desu* pattern sometimes
causes confusion.

Formula

N1 wa V N2 desu.

N1 is N2 who does V.

N1 = a noun acting as the subject of the sentence

V = a verb in plain present, plain past, or plain present progressive tense that is placed before a noun

N2 = a noun that provides information about the subject and is modified by a verb

Polite

10時に来る人は朝日銀行の小林さんです。

Jū-ji ni kuru hito wa Asahi Ginkō no Kobayashi-san desu.

The person who is coming at 10:00 is Mr. Kobayashi of Asahi Bank.

今電話をしている男の人は、課長です。

Ima denwa o shite iru otoko no hito wa, kachō desu.

The man who is talking on the phone is the section manager.

この小説を書いた作家を知っていますか。

Kono shōsetsu o kaita sakka o shitte imasu ka.

Do you know the writer who wrote this novel?

Informal

BETWEEN WOMEN

中川：明日の会議に出る人は、誰？

Nakagawa: Ashita no kaigi ni deru hito wa, dare?

Who is going to attend tomorrow's meeting?

黒田：佐藤さんと私よ。

Kuroda: Satō-san to watashi yo.

Mr. Sato and myself.

久子：フランスで買ってきた洋服って、これ？

Hisako: Furansu de katte kita yōfuku tte, kore?

Are these the clothes you bought in France?

俊子：そうよ。いいでしょう？

Toshiko: Sō yo. Ii deshō?

That right. Nice, aren't they?

> Variation **1** Negative Verb Modifying Noun (*V-nai N*)
>
> ## <u>N1</u> は <u>V</u> ない <u>N2</u> です。
>
> *N1 wa V-nai N2 desu.*
> N1 is N2 who doesn't do V.
>
> ## この人達はあまり勉強しない学生です。
>
> *Kono hito-tachi wa amari benkyō shinai gakusei desu.*
> These are the students who don't study very much.

This variation is essentially the same as Basic Pattern 44 (*<u>N1</u> wa <u>V</u> <u>N2</u> desu*) except that the verb modifying the noun is in a negative form. The verbs can be in the plain present, plain past, or plain present progressive (*-te iru*) tense.

 Formula

<u>N1</u> wa <u>V</u>-nai <u>N2</u> desu.

N1 is N2 who doesn't do V.

N1 = a noun acting as the subject of the sentence

V = the negative form of a verb in the plain present, plain past, or plain present progressive tense

N2 = a noun that provides information about the subject and is modified by a verb

日曜日のパーティに出ない人は誰ですか。

Nichiyōbi no pātī ni denai hito wa dare desu ka?

Who is not going to attend Sunday's party?

雨が降らない日にドライブに行きましょう。

Ame ga furanai hi ni doraibu ni ikimashō.

Let's go driving on a day when it doesn't rain / when it's not raining.

BETWEEN MEN

沢井：まだ仕事が終わっていない人は、明日続けてやってほしいんだけど。

Sawai: Mada shigoto ga owatte inai hito wa, ashita tsuzukete yatte hoshii 'n da kedo.

I'd like those who haven't finished their work yet to continue with it tomorrow.

松木：でも明日は土曜日だよ。

Matsuki: Demo ashita wa doyōbi da yo.

But tomorrow is Saturday, you know.

BETWEEN WOMEN

美佐子：雨が降ってきたけど、傘もってこなかった人いる？

Misako: Ame ga futte kita kedo, kasa motte konakatta hito iru?

It's started to rain. Is there anyone who didn't bring an umbrella?

波子：みんな持ってきたわ。

Namiko: Minna motte kita wa.

Everybody brought one.

Ｎが/はＶそうです。

N ga / wa V sō desu.

It is said that N does V.

来週米国の大統領が来日するそうです。

Raishū Beikoku no daitōryō ga rainichi suru sō desu.

I hear that the president of the United States is coming to Japan next week.

This pattern is used to convey information that one has heard from another party. A plain-form verb in the present, past, or present progressive (*-te iru*) tense precedes *sō* ("that is what [I hear]").

Formula

N ga / wa V sō desu.

It is said that N does V.

N = a noun acting as the subject of the sentence

V = a plain-form verb in the present, past, or present progrssive (*-te iru*) tense followed by *sō desu*

Polite

大塚：ずいぶん道が混んでいますね。

Ōtsuka: Zuibun michi ga konde imasu ne.

The streets are really crowded, aren't they.

亀井：ええ、少し前に事故があったそうですよ。

Kamei: Ee, sukoshi mae ni jiko ga atta sō desu yo.

Yes, I hear there was an accident a little while ago.

BETWEEN WOMEN

文子：明日のコンサートに裕子を誘わない？

Fumiko: Ashita no konsāto ni Hiroko o sasowanai?

Shall we invite Hiroko to tomorrow's concert?

幸恵：だめ、裕子はゴルフに行くそうよ。

Sachie: Dame, Hiroko wa gorufu ni iku sō yo.

That's no good. I hear Hiroko's going golfing.

Variation 1 Expressing Negative Hearsay (*V-nai sō*)

N が / は **V** ないそうです。

N ga / wa V-nai sō desu.

It is said that N does not do V.

明日は雨は降らないそうです。

Ashita wa ame wa furanai sō desu.

They say that it won't rain tomorrow.

This is the negative version of Basic Pattern 45 (<u>N</u> *ga* / *wa* <u>V</u> *sō desu*). The difference is that the verb preceding *sō* is in the plain negative form.

Formula

<u>N</u> ga / wa <u>V</u>-nai sō desu.

It is said that N does not do V.

N = a noun acting as the subject of the sentence

V = a negative plain-form verb in the present, past, or present progressive (*-te iru*) tense followed by *sō desu*

片山：社長はいつアメリカから帰ってくるんですか。

Katayama: Shachō wa itsu Amerika kara kaette kuru 'n desu ka.

When will the president be coming back from the United States?

内山：さあ、よくわかりませんが、今週はまだ帰ってこないそうですよ。

Uchiyama: Saa, yoku wakarimasen ga, konshū wa mada kaette konai sō desu yo.

Well, I don't know exactly, but I hear he won't be coming back this week.

BETWEEN MEN

川村：久保君、就職決まったのかな。

Kawamura: Kubo-kun, shūshoku kimatta no ka na.

I wonder if Kubo has landed a job.

伊東：まだ決まっていないそうだよ。

Itō: Mada kimatte inai sō da yo.

So far I hear there's nothing definite.

Basic Pattern **46** Conjecturing and Making Suppositions (*V-sō*)

Nが / は**V**そうです。　　雨が降りそうです。

N ga / wa V-sō desu.　　*Ame ga furisō desu.*

N looks as though it might V.　It looks like rain.

Whereas Basic Pattern 45 (*N ga / wa V sō desu*) conveys tentative information based on what one has heard, this pattern conveys tentative information based on what one has seen or observed. The verb is formed by adding *sō* to the *masu* stem (the *masu* form of a verb minus *masu*).

<u>N</u> ga / wa <u>V</u>-sō desu.
N looks as though it might V.
N = a noun acting as the subject of the sentence
V = a *masu*-stem verb to which *sō* has been added

来週は円が下がりそうです。

Raishū wa en ga sagarisō desu.
It looks as though the yen will go down next week.

桜の花がもうすぐ咲きそうです。

Sakura no hana ga mō sugu sakisō desu.
The cherry trees look as though they are about to bloom.

BETWEEN WOMEN

加奈子：このホテル大きいわね。私達の部屋 はどこ？

Kanako: Kono hoteru ōkii wa ne. Watashi-tachi no heya wa doko?
What a big hotel. Where's our room?

朝子：部屋へ行くのに迷いそう。

Asako: Heya e iku no ni mayoisō.
It looks like we might get lost on the way to our room.

<u>N</u>が / は <u>V</u> ようです。

N ga / wa V yō desu.

N seems as though it will do V.

週末台風がくるようです。

Shūmatsu taifū ga kuru yō desu.

It seems that a typoon is coming this weekend.

This variation expresses supposition based on reliable information and the speaker's evaluation of it. It is formed by placing a plain-form verb in the present, past, or present progressive (*-te iru*) tense before *yō desu*

Formula

<u>N</u> ga / wa <u>V</u> yō desu.

N seems as though it will do V.

N = a noun acting as the subject of the sentence

V = a plain-form verb in the present, past, or present progressive (*-te iru*) tense followed by *yō desu*

Polite

持田：冬のボーナスは出ますか。

Mochida: Fuyu no bōnasu wa demasu ka.

Will we be getting a winter bonus?

大竹：課長の話では、出るようですよ。

Ōtake: Kachō no hanashi de wa, deru yō desu yo.

According to the section manager, it seems we will.

BETWEEN MEN

森田：今晩、金子も飲みに行くのかな。

Morita: Konban, Kaneko mo nomi ni iku no ka na.

I wonder if Kaneko is also going out drinking tonight.

高橋：行くようだよ。もう仕事終わったよう
だから。

Takahashi: Iku yō da yo. Mō shigoto owatta yō da kara.

It seems he's going since he appears to have finished his
work.

| Variation **2** | Conjecturing and Making Suppositions (*V rashii*) |

Nが / は **V** らしいです。

N ga / wa V rashii desu.

N seems to be V.

先生は旅行に行くらしいです。

Sensei wa ryokō ni iku rashii desu.

It seems that the teacher is going on a trip.

This variation is quite similar to Variation 1 in that it represents a supposition made by the speaker. The possible
sources of information are broad, including what has been
heard, seen, or read. *Rashii* follows plain-form verbs in the
present, past, or present progressive (*-te iru*) tense (affir-
mative or negative), as well as nouns and adjectives.

Formula

N ga / wa V rashii desu.

N seems to be V.

N = a noun acting as the subject of the sentence

V = a verb in the present, past, or present progressive (*-te iru*) tense followed by *rashii desu*

外務大臣は来週からフランスへ行くらしいです。

Gaimu-daijin wa raishū kara Furansu e iku rashii desu.

It seems that the Foreign Minister will go to France next week.

週末は雨が降るらしいです。

Shūmatsu wa ame ga furu rashii desu.

It seems that it'll rain on the weekend.

BETWEEN WOMEN

高木：来学期英語の先生やめるの知ってる？

Takagi: Raigakki Eigo no sensei yameru no shitte 'ru?

Did you know the English teacher's quitting next semester?

吉岡：聞いたわ。結婚するらしいよ。

Yoshioka: Kiita wa. Kekkon suru rashii yo.

Yes, I heard. It seems she's getting married.

Basic Pattern 47

This chapter introduces the subjunctive mood ("if") of verbs, with several variations. In many cases, these patterns are interchangable with little change in meaning, but even then each retains a core meaning that is different from the others. We will try to point out a few of these differences in core meaning. For adjective and noun sentences in the subjunctive mood, see Basic Pattern 15.

Basic Pattern 47 **The Subjunctive with *V-tara***

(もし) N1 が V1 たら (N2 は) N3 です / V2 ます。
(Moshi) N1 ga V1-tara (N2 wa) N3 desu / V2-masu.
If N1 does V1, (N2) is N3 / does V2.

(もし) 雨が降ったら延ばします。
(Moshi) ame ga futtara nobashimasu.
If it rains, we'll do it another time.

This pattern shows the subjunctive mood with verbs ending in *tara*. The verb is formed by adding *ra* to the plain past tense (e.g., *tabeta* becomes *tabetara*). While the general meaning is "if," the core meaning is "supposing that" or "if … should happen." Placing *moshi* ("if") at the head of the sentence is optional. The subject of the sentence-ending verb (N2) is often omitted as being understood.

Formula

(Moshi) <u>N1</u> ga <u>V1</u>-tara (N2 wa) <u>N3</u> desu / <u>V2</u>-masu.
If N1 does V1, (N2) is N3 / does V2.

N1 = a noun acting as the subject of the verb in *tara* form
V1 = a verb in the *tara* form
N2 = a noun acting as the subject of the sentence
N3 = a noun providing information about the subject of the sentence
V2 = a sentence-ending verb providing information about the subject of the sentence

---

Polite

青木：機械が故障したらどうしましょうか。
Aoki: Kikai ga koshō shitara dō shimashō ka.
If the machine breaks down, what should I do?

工藤：故障したら私に電話を下さい。
Kudō: Koshō shitara watashi ni denwa o kudasai.
If it breaks down, please call me.

Informal

BETWEEN MEN

市川：雪が降ったら電車で行こう。
Ichikawa: Yuki ga futtara densha de ikō.
If it snows, let's go by train.

富田：スノー・タイヤをつけたら大丈夫だろう。

Tomita: Sunō-taiya o tsuketara daijōbu darō.

If we put on snow tires, it should be all right.

Variation **1** The Subjunctive with *V-ba*

(もし) <u>N1</u>が<u>V1</u>ば (<u>N2</u>は) <u>N3</u>です / <u>V2</u>ます。

(Moshi) N1 ga V1-ba (N2 wa) N3 desu / V2-masu.

If N1 does V1, (N2) is N3 / does V2.

(もし) 余分の切符があれば友達を誘います。

(Moshi) yobun no kippu ga areba tomodachi o sasoimasu.

If there's an extra ticket, I'll invite a friend.

This variation indicates the subjunctive mood ("if") in the *ba* form. Though it can have both hypothetical and conditional meanings, its main emphasis resides in the conditional ("providing that …," "on the condition that"). For formation of the *ba* form, refer to the Verb Conjugation Chart at the end of the book or see my *Japanese Verbs at a Glance*.

Formula

(Moshi) <u>N1</u> ga <u>V1</u>-ba (<u>N2</u> wa) <u>N3</u> desu / <u>V2</u>-masu.

If N1 does V1, (N2) is N3 / does V2.

N1 = a noun acting as the subject of the verb in *ba* form

V1 = a verb in the *ba* form

N2 = a noun acting as the subject of the sentence

N3 = a noun providing information about the subject of the sentence

V2 = a sentence-ending verb providing information about the subject of the sentence

山本：今この株を買えば、どのくらい利益が
ありますか。

Yamamoto: Ima kono kabu o kaeba, dono kurai rieki ga arimasu ka.

How much profit will there be if we buy this stock now?

吉田：さあ、はっきりわかりませんが、かな
りあると思いますよ。

Yoshida: Sā, hakkiri wakarimasen ga, kanari aru to omoi-masu yo.

Well, I don't know exactly, but I think it would be considerable.

BETWEEN MEN

斉藤：新しいパソコン買ったんだけど、使い
方覚えられないよ。

Saitō: Atarashii pasokon katta 'n da kedo, tsukaikata oboe-rarenai yo.

I bought a new PC, but I can't figure out how to use it.

横田：大丈夫、2、3週間たてば、覚えられるよ。

Yokota: Daijōbu, ni, san-shūkan tateba, oboerareru yo.

Don't worry. In two or three weeks you'll figure it out.

BETWEEN WOMEN

久子：明日のパーティ、行く？

Hisako: Ashita no pāti, iku?

Are you going to the party tomorrow?

友恵：行かない。久子は？

Tomoe: Ikanai. Hisako wa?

I'm not going. How about you?

久子：友恵が行かなければ、私も行かない。
Hisako: Tomoe ga ikanakereba, watashi mo ikanai.
If you're not going, I'm not either.

This pattern can also be used to express regret and disappointment.

こんな所へ来なければ良かった。
Konna tokoro e konakereba yokatta.
I wish I hadn't come to a place like this.

Variation ❷ The Subjunctive with *to*

(<u>N1 は/が</u>) <u>V1</u> と (<u>N2 は/が</u>) <u>N3</u> です / <u>V2</u> ます。
(N1 wa/ga) V1 to (N2 wa/ga) N3 desu / V2-masu.
If N1 does V1, N2 is N3 / does V2.

お金を入れてこのボタンを押すと切符が出てきます。
Okane o irete kono botan o osu to kippu ga dete kimasu.
If you insert a coin and press this button, a ticket comes out.

While this variation indicates the subjunctive mood ("if"), both hypothetical and conditional, the nuance is that if (or when) one thing happens, then something else will happen *without fail*. It is formed by a plain-form verb preceding the particle *to*. In translation, *to* seems to vary between "if" and "when." While Basic Pattern 47 and Variation 1 can end with a command (i.e., "If this happens, don't do that"), this pattern cannot. In the formula for this pattern, the subject of the verb preceding *to*, and the subject of *N3 desu* or *V2-masu* can be the same or different, and they can be expressed or not expressed, depending on context.

(N1 wa/ga) V1 to (N2 wa/ga) N3 desu / V2-masu.
If N1 does V1, N2 is N3 / does V2.
N1 = a noun acting as the subject of the verb preceding *to*
V1 = verb in present plain form preceding *to*
N2 = a noun acting as a subject of the sentence
N3 = a noun providing information about the subject
V2 = a verb providing information about the subject

Polite

山本：こんなに雨が降らないと、また水不足
ですね。

Yamamoto: Konna ni ame ga furanai to, mata mizu-busoku desu ne.

If it continues not raining like this, we'll have another water shortage.

鈴木：本当に、困りますね。

Suzuki: Hontō ni, komarimasu ne.

We'll be in a fix all right.

Informal

BETWEEN WOMEN

浪江：ローマ字をひらがなに変えるの、どう
するの？

Namie: Rōmaji o hiragana ni kaeru no, dō suru no?

How can I change romanization into *hiragana*?

多美：このキー押すと、ひらがなになるわ。

Tami: Kono kī osu to, hiragana ni naru wa.

If you push this key, you get *hiragana*.

This pattern also indicates that if you do one thing, you will discover, or come across, something new.

次の交差点を右に曲がると、教会があります。

Tsugi no kōsa-ten o migi ni magaru to, kyōkai ga arimasu.

If you turn to the right at the next intersection, you'll
   find a church.

Basic Patterns 48-50

This chapter deals with three types of passive forms, in which something is done to the subject of the sentence. One of these forms is similar to the English passive but two are not, being derived from intransitive verbs. In addition, two types of causative verbs are discussed, in which the subject *makes* others do something. By contrast, in the causative-passive form, the final pattern in the book, the subject *is made to do* something.

Basic Pattern 48 Direct Passive (*N ni [trans] V[passive]-masu*)

<u>N1</u> は <u>N2</u> に <u>V</u> (passive) ます。

N1 wa N2 ni V(passive)-masu.

N1 is V-ed by N2.

山は雪に覆われます。

Yama wa yuki ni ōwaremasu.

The mountains are covered by the snow.

This pattern makes use of passive verb forms (i.e., verbs that indicate that the subject is on the receiving end of the action expressed by the verb). A simple example in English would be, "John was bitten by a dog." This form makes use of a transitive verb (a verb that takes a direct object) and is called the direct passive. Its Japanese and English forms are fairly similar. In Japanese, the doer of the action that effects the subject of the sentence is followed by the particle *ni*. For information about how passive verbs are formed, see the Verb Conjugation Chart at the back of this book or my *Japanese Verbs at a Glance.*

Formula

N1 wa N2 ni V(passive)-masu.

N1 is V-ed by N2.

N1 = a noun acting as the subject of the sentence, representing the receiver of the action

N2 = a noun representing the doer or agent of the action, followed by the particle *ni*

V = a transitive verb in passive form plus *masu, te imasu,* or *mashita*

Polite

子供はお母さんに叱られました。

Kodomo wa okāsan ni shikararemashita.

The child was scolded by its mother.

その新聞は会社員によく読まれています。

Sono shinbun wa kaisha-in ni yoku yomarete imasu.

That newspaper is widely read by white-collar workers.

BETWEEN GIRLS

友恵：コンサート終わったら、歌手にサイン
　　してもらわない？

Tomoe: Konsāto owattara, kashu ni sain shite morawanai?

Why don't we get the singer's autograph after the concert?

緑：無理よ。彼いつも大勢のフアンに囲まれ
　　てるから。

Midori: Muri yo. Kare itsumo ōzei no fuan ni kakomarete 'ru kara.

That's impossible. He's always surrounded by hordes of fans.

| Variation | 1 | Indirect Passive (*N ni [intrans] V[passive]-masu*) |

N1 は N2 に V (passive) ます。

N1 wa N2 ni V(passive)-masu.

N1 is V-ed by N2.

私は雨に降られました。

Watashi wa ame ni furaremashita.

I was rained on.

This variation occurs with the passive form of an intransitive verb (a verb that does not take a direct object) and is called the indirect passive. Most verbs in the indirect passive form express suffering or discomfiture on the speaker's part that is caused by external actions or happenings. It is often difficult to translate this type of sentence exactly into English because of the differences in intransitive verb usage.

_N1_ wa _N2_ ni _V(passive)_-masu.

N1 is V-ed by N2.

N1 = a noun acting as the subject of the sentence, representing the receiver of the action

N2 = a noun representing the doer or agent of the action followed by particle _ni_

V = an intransitive verb in passive form plus _masu, te imasu,_ or _mashita_

この戦争で、息子に死なれた母親が多くいます。

Kono sensō de, musuko ni shinareta hahaoya ga ōku imasu.

There are many mothers whose sons were killed in this war.

昨日の晩遅く友達に来られて、勉強が出来ませんでした。

Kinō no ban osoku tomodachi ni korarete, benkyō ga deki-masen deshita.

Some friends visited me quite late last night, so I couldn't study at all.

BETWEEN WOMEN

川島：週末楽しかった？

Kawashima: Shūmatsu tanoshikatta?

Did you have a nice weekend?

松木：伊豆へドライブに行ったのに、雨に降られてがっかりだったわ。

Matsuki: Izu e doraibu ni itta no ni, ame ni furarete gakkari datta wa.

I went driving to Izu but got rained on. What a disappointment!

N1 は N2 に N3 を V (passive) ます。

N1 wa N2 ni N3 o V(passive)-masu.

N1 is V-ed N3 by N2.

私は泥棒にカメラを盗まれました。

Watashi wa dorobō ni kamera o nusumaremashita.

I had my camera stolen by a thief.

This pattern is the indirect passive form and the same as Variation 1 except that the verb takes an object, which is something that does not occur in English. It expresses suffering or discomfiture on the speaker's part that is caused by external actions or happenings.

Formula

N1 wa N2 ni N3 o V(passive)-masu.

N1 is V-ed N3 by N2.

N1 = a noun acting as the subject of the sentence, representing the receiver of the action

N2 = a noun representing the doer or agent of the action, followed by particle *ni*

N3 = a noun acting as the direct object of the passive verb

V = a transitive verb in passive form plus *masu, te imasu,* or *mashita*

Polite

私は猫に大切な茶碗を壊されてしまいました。

Watashi wa neko ni taisetsu na chawan o kowasarete shi-maimashita.

I had a precious tea cup broken by my cat.

その子供は隣の犬に手をかまれました。

Sono kodomo wa tonari no inu ni te o kamaremashita.

That child had its hand bitten by the neighbor's dog.

Informal

BETWEEN WOMEN

菅原：ボーイフレンドの写真、母に見られち
ゃった。

Sugawara: Bōi-furendo no shashin, haha ni mirarechatta.

The picture of my boyfriend was seen by my mother.

大西：お母さん知らなかったから、びっくり
したでしょうね。

Ōnishi: Okāsan shiranakatta kara, bikkuri shita deshō ne.

She must have been surprised since she didn't know about
him.

Basic Pattern **49** Causative (*N o/ni V[causative]-masu*)

<u>N1</u> は / が <u>N2</u> を / に <u>V</u> (causative) ます。

N1 wa / ga N2 o / ni V(causative)-masu.

N1 makes N2 do V.

社長は社員を夜遅くまで働かせます。

Shachō wa shain o yoru osoku made hatarakasemasu.

The company president makes the employees work
until late at night.

This pattern is used in situations where the subject of the
sentence forces others to do something. The verb is in the
causative form. In translation, the causative form seems to
range in meaning from "force" to "make" and "have." The
noun showing who is being forced is followed by the particle

ni or *o*. For examples of how to conjugate the causative verb form, see the Verb Conjugation Chart at the back of this book.

<u>N1</u> wa / ga <u>N2</u> o / ni <u>V</u>(causative)-masu.

N1 makes N2 do V.

N1 = a noun acting as the subject of the sentence, representing the doer or agent of the action

N2 = a noun representing who is being forced, followed by the particle *ni* or *o*

V = verb in causative form plus *masu*, *te imasu*, or *mashita*

◖ **Polite** ◗ ────────────────────────

先生は学生を帰らせます。

Sensei wa gakusei o kaerasemasu.
The teacher makes the students go home.

私は毎朝犬を散歩させます。

Watashi wa maiasa inu o sampo sasemasu.
Every morning I walk my dog.

◖ **Informal** ◗ ────────────────────────

BETWEEN MEN

北岡：空港へ行く人は僕一人？

Kitaoka: Kūkō e iku hito wa boku hitori?
Am I the only one going to the airport?

後藤：いや、荷物があるから武田君も行かせるよ。

Gotō: Iya, nimotsu ga aru kara Takeda-kun mo ikaseru yo.
No, I'll have Takeda go too, since you have luggage.

<u>N1</u> は / が <u>N2</u> を / に <u>N3</u> を <u>V</u>(causative) ます。

N1 wa / ga N2 o / ni N3 o V(causative)-masu.
N1 makes N2 do V N3.

医者は患者に薬を飲ませます。

Isha wa kanja ni kusuri o nomasemasu.
The doctor makes his patients take medicine.

This pattern is essentially the same as Basic Pattern 49 except that the sentence-ending verb takes a direct object. The subject of the sentence forces others to do something. The verb is a transitive verb in the causative form. In translation, the causative form seems to range from "force" to "make" and "have." The noun showing who is being forced is followed by the particle *ni* or *o*.

Formula

N1 wa / ga <u>N2</u> o / ni <u>N3</u> o <u>V</u>(causative)-masu.

N1 makes N2 do V N3.

N1 = a noun acting as the subject of the sentence, representing the doer or agent of the action

N2 = a noun representing who is being forced, followed by the particle *ni* or *o*

N3 = a noun that is the direct object of the sentence-ending verb

V = a sentence-ending verb in causative form plus *masu, te imasu,* or *mashita*

お母さんは子供にご飯を食べさせています。

Okāsan wa kodomo ni gohan o tabesasete imasu.

The mother is feeding her child.

先生は学生にレポートを書かせました。

Sensei wa gakusei ni repōto o kakasemashita.

The teacher had the students write reports.

Informal

BETWEEN WOMEN

池田：買い物がたくさんある時、どうなさるの？

Ikeda: Kaimono ga takusan aru toki, dō nasaru no?

What do you do when you have a lot of things you bought?

石井：息子に車を運転させて行くのよ。

Ishii: Musuko ni kuruma o unten sasete iku no yo.

I have my son drive me.

Basic Pattern 50 Causative Passive (*N ni V[causative-passive]-masu*)

<u>N1</u> は <u>N2</u> に <u>V</u> (causative-passive) ます。

N1 wa N2 ni V(causative-passive)-masu.

N1 is made to do V by N2.

社員は社長に夜遅くまで働かされます。

Shain wa shachō ni yoru osoku made hatarakasaremasu.

Employees are made to work until late at night by the
company president.

This pattern expresses a causative-passive situation: that is,
a situation in which the subject of the sentence is forced to
do something by another. The verb is a combination of

causative and passive forms, examples of which can be found in the Verb Conjugation Chart at the back of the book.

❮ Formula ❯

N1 *wa* N2 *ni* V(causative-passive)-masu.

N1 is made to do V by N2.

N1 = a noun acting as the subject of the sentence, representing the receiver of the action

N2 = a noun representing who is doing the forcing, followed by the particle *ni*

V = a verb in causative-passive form plus *masu, te imasu,* or *mashita*

❮ Polite ❯

私は病院で1時間以上も待たされます／待たせられます。

Watashi wa byōin de, ichi-jikan ijō mo matasaremasu / mataseraremasu.

I have to wait more than an hour at the hospital.

電車の事故で、一駅歩かされました／歩かせられました。

Densha no jiko de, hito-eki arukasaremashita / arukaseraremashita.

Because of the train accident we were forced to walk from one station to the next.

You can see from the above examples that there are two ways of making causative passive forms for some verbs. See the Verb Conjugation Chart at the back of the book.

BETWEEN WOMEN

岡本：いい映画だったわね

Okamoto: Ii eiga datta wa ne.

It was a good movie, wasn't it.

木村：本当。こういう映画見ると、将来のこと考えさせられるわね。

Kimura: Hontō. Kō iu eiga miru to, shōrai no koto kangaesaserareru wa ne.

Really. Seeing a movie like that makes you think about the future.

Variation 1 Causative Passive (*N ni N o V[causative-passive]-masu*)

<u>N1</u> は <u>N2</u> に <u>N3</u> を <u>V</u>(causative-passive)ます。

N1 wa N2 ni N3 o V(causative-passive)-masu.

N1 is made to do V N3 by N2.

社員は社長に夜遅くまで仕事をさせられます。

Shain wa shachō ni yoru osoku made shigoto o saseraremasu.

Employees are kept working until late at night by the president of the company.

This causative-passive variation is the same as Basic Pattern 50 (<u>*N1*</u> *wa* <u>*N2*</u> *ni* <u>*V*</u>*[causative-passive]-masu*) except that the verb takes a direct object. It describes a situation in which the subject of the sentence is forced to do something by another party. The verb is a combination of causative and passive forms, examples of which can be found in the Verb Conjugation Chart at the back of the book.

N1 wa *N2* ni *N3* o *V(causative-passive)-masu.*

N1 is made to do V N3 by N2.

N1 = a noun acting as the subject of the sentence, representing the receiver of the action

N2 = a noun representing who is doing the forcing, followed by the particle *ni*

N3 = a noun acting as the direct object of the sentence-ending verb, followed by *o*

V = a verb in causative-passive form plus *masu, te imasu,* or *mashita*

園田：昨日の晩はどこへ行ったんですか。

Sonoda: Kinō no ban wa doko e itta 'n desu ka.

Where did you go last night?

高村：カラオケへ行って、友達に歌を歌わせられました。

Takamura: Karaoke e itte, tomodachi ni uta o utawase-raremashita.

I went to a karaoke bar, where a friend forced me to sing.

BETWEEN GIRLS

泉：何買ったの？

Izumi: Nani katta no?

What did you buy?

片山：高い化粧品買わされちゃった。

Katayama: Takai keshō-hin kawasarechatta.

I was forced (persuaded) to buy some expensive cosmetics.

Appendices

Verb Conjugation Chart

Group 1 ——————————————————————————————

plain form	-*masu* form	-*te* form	-*nai* form	-*ta* form	-*ba* form
agaru 上がる rise, go up	*agarimasu* 上がります	*agatte* 上がって	*agaranai* 上がらない	*agatta* 上がった	*agareba* 上がれば
aku 開く open (i)	*akimasu* 開きます	*aite* 開いて	*akanai* 開かない	*aita* 開いた	*akeba* 開けば
arau 洗う wash	*araimasu* 洗います	*aratte* 洗って	*arawanai* 洗わない	*aratta* 洗った	*araeba* 洗えば
aru ある exist	*arimasu* あります	*atte* あって	*nai* ない	*atta* あった	*areba* あれば
aruku 歩く walk	*arukimasu* 歩きます	*aruite* 歩いて	*arukanai* 歩かない	*aruita* 歩いた	*arukeba* 歩けば
asobu 遊ぶ play	*asobimasu* 遊びます	*asonde* 遊んで	*asobanai* 遊ばない	*asonda* 遊んだ	*asobeba* 遊べば
atsumaru 集まる get together (i)	*atsumarimasu* 集まります	*atsumatte* 集まって	*atsumaranai* 集まらない	*atsumatta* 集まった	*atsumareba* 集まれば
au 会う meet	*aimasu* 会います	*atte* 会って	*awanai* 会わない	*atta* 会った	*aeba* 会えば
dasu 出す take out, put out (t)	*dashimasu* 出します	*dashite* 出して	*dasanai* 出さない	*dashita* 出した	*daseba* 出せば
erabu 選ぶ choose	*erabimasu* 選びます	*erande* 選んで	*erabanai* 選ばない	*eranda* 選んだ	*erabeba* 選べば
furu 降る rain, snow	*furimasu* 降ります	*futte* 降って	*furanai* 降らない	*futta* 降った	*fureba* 降れば

conditional	potential	volitional	passive	causative
agattara 上ったら	*agareru* 上がれる	*agarō* 上がろう	*agarareru* 上がられる	*agaraseru* 上がらせる
aitara 開いたら	— —	*akō* 開こう	— —	— —
arattara 洗ったら	*araeru* 洗える	*araō* 洗おう	*arawareru* 洗われる	*arawaseru* 洗わせる
attara あったら	— —	arō あろう	— —	— —
aruitara 歩いたら	*arukeru* 歩ける	*arukō* 歩こう	*arukareru* 歩かれる	*arukaseru* 歩かせる
asondara 遊んだら	*asoberu* 遊べる	*asobō* 遊ぼう	*asobareru* 遊ばれる	*asobaseru* 遊ばせる
atsumattara 集まったら	*atsumareru* 集まれる	*atsumarō* 集まろう	*atsumareru* 集まれる	*atsumaraseru* 集まらせる
attara 会ったら	*aeru* 会える	*aō* 会おう	*awareru* 会われる	*awaseru* 会わせる
dashitara 出したら	*daseru* 出せる	*dasō* 出そう	*dasareru* 出される	*dasaseru* 出させる
erandara 選んだら	*eraberu* 選べる	*erabō* 選ぼう	*erabareru* 選ばれる	*erabaseru* 選ばせる
futtara 降ったら	— —	*furō* 降ろう	*furareru* 降られる	*furaseru* 降らせる

plain form	-*masu* form	-*te* form	-*nai* form	-*ta* form	-*ba* form
hairu 入る enter (i)	*hairimasu* 入ります	*haitte* 入って	*hairanai* 入らない	*haitta* 入った	*haireba* 入れば
hajimaru 始まる start (i)	*hajimarimasu* 始まります	*hajimatte* 始まって	*hajimaranai* 始まらない	*hajimatta* 始まった	*hajimareba* 始まれば
herasu 減らす decrease (t)	*herashimasu* 減らします	*herashite* 減らして	*herasanai* 減らさない	*herashita* 減らした	*heraseba* 減らせば
heru 減る decrease (i)	*herimasu* 減ります	*hette* 減って	*heranai* 減らない	*hetta* 減った	*hereba* 減れば
hiku 引く pull	*hikimasu* 引きます	*hiite* 引いて	*hikanai* 引かない	*hiita* 引いた	*hikeba* 引けば
iku 行く go	*ikimasu* 行きます	*itte* 行って	*ikanai* 行かない	*itta* 行った	*ikeba* 行けば
iu (yū) 言う say	*iimasu* 言います	*itte (yutte)* 言って	*iwanai* 言わない	*itta (yutta)* 言った	*ieba* 言えば
kaeru 帰る return	*kaerimasu* 帰ります	*kaette* 帰って	*kaeranai* 帰らない	*kaetta* 帰った	*kaereba* 帰れば
kaku 描く、書く draw, write	*kakimasu* 書きます	*kaite* 書いて	*kakanai* 書かない	*kaita* 書いた	*kakeba* 書けば
kasu 貸す lend	*kashimasu* 貸します	*kashite* 貸して	*kasanai* 貸さない	*kashita* 貸した	*kaseba* 貸せば
kau 買う buy	*kaimasu* 買います	*katte* 買って	*kawanai* 買わない	*katta* 買った	*kaeba* 買えば
kawakasu 乾かす dry (t)	*kawakashimasu* 乾かします	*kawakashite* 乾かして	*kawakasanai* 乾かさない	*kawakashita* 乾かした	*kawakaseba* 乾かせば
kawaku 乾く dry (i)	*kawakimasu* 乾きます	*kawaite* 乾いて	*kawakasanai* 乾かない	*kawaita* 乾いた	*kawakeba* 乾けば

conditional	potential	volitional	passive	causative
haittara 入ったら	*haireru* 入れる	*hairō* 入ろう	*hairareru* 入られる	*hairaseru* 入らせる
hajimattara 始まったら	— —	*hajimarō* 始まろう	— —	— —
herashitara 減らしたら	*heraseru* 減らせる	*herasō* 減らそう	*herasareru* 減らされる	*herasaseru* 減らさせる
hettara 減ったら	— —	*herō* 減ろう	— —	— —
hiitara 引いたら	*hikeru* 引ける	*hikō* 引こう	*hikareru* 引かれる	*hikaseru* 引かせる
ittara 行ったら	*ikeru* 行ける	*ikō* 行こう	*ikareru* 行かれる	*ikaseru* 行かせる
ittara (yuttara) 言ったら	*ieru* 言える	*iō* 言おう	*iwareru* 言われる	*iwaseru* 言わせる
kaettara 帰ったら	*kaerareru* 帰れる	*kaerō* 帰ろう	*kaerareru* 帰られる	*kaeraseru* 帰らせる
kaitara 書いたら	*kakeru* 書ける	*kakō* 書こう	*kakareru* 書かれる	*kakaseru* 書かせる
kashitara 貸したら	*kaseru* 貸せる	*kasō* 貸そう	*kasareru* 貸される	*kasaseru* 貸させる
kattara 買ったら	*kaeru* 買える	*kaō* 買おう	*kawareru* 買われる	*kawaseru* 買わせる
kawakashitara 乾かしたら	*kawakaseru* 乾かせる	*kawakasō* 乾かそう	*kawakasareru* 乾かされる	*kawakasaseru* 乾かさせる
kawaitara 乾いたら	— —	*kawakō* 乾こう	— —	— —

plain form	*-masu* form	*-te* form	*-nai* form	*-ta* form	*-ba* form
kesu 消す put out fire, turn off light (t)	*keshimasu* 消します	*keshite* 消して	*kesanai* 消さない	*keshita* 消した	*keseba* 消せば
kiku 聞く listen	*kikimasu* 聞きます	*kiite* 聞いて	*kikanai* 聞かない	*kiita* 聞いた	*kikeba* 聞けば
kimaru 決まる decide (i)	*kimarimasu* 決まります	*kimatte* 決って	*kimaranai* 決まらない	*kimatta* 決まった	*kimareba* 決まれば
kiru 切る cut	*kirimasu* 切ります	*kitte* 切って	*kiranai* 切らない	*kitta* 切った	*kireba* 切れば
komu 混む be crowded	*komimasu* 混みます	*konde* 混んで	*komanai* 混まない	*konda* 混んだ	*komeba* 混めば
korosu 殺す kill	*koroshimasu* 殺します	*koroshite* 殺して	*korosanai* 殺さない	*koroshita* 殺した	*koroseba* 殺せば
matsu 待つ wait	*machimasu* 待ちます	*matte* 待って	*matanai* 待たない	*matta* 待った	*mateba* 待てば
motsu 持つ have, hold	*mochimasu* 持ちます	*motte* 持って	*motanai* 持たない	*motta* 持った	*moteba* 持てば
naku 泣く cry	*nakimasu* 泣きます	*naite* 泣いて	*nakanai* 泣かない	*naita* 泣いた	*nakeba* 泣けば
naoru 直る recover, be fixed (i)	*naorimasu* 直ります	*naotte* 直って	*naoranai* 直らない	*naotta* 直った	*naoreba* 直れば
naosu 直す fix, mend (t)	*naoshimasu* 直します	*naoshite* 直して	*naosanai* 直さない	*naoshita* 直した	*naoseba* 直せば
narau 習う learn	*naraimasu* 習います	*naratte* 習って	*narawanai* 習わない	*naratta* 習った	*naraeba* 習えば
naru なる become	*narimasu* なります	*natte* なって	*naranai* ならない	*natta* なった	*nareba* なれば

conditional	potential	volitional	passive	causative
keshitara 消したら	*keseru* 消せる	*kesō* 消そう	*kesareru* 消される	*kesaseru* 消させる
kiitara 聞いたら	*kikeru* 聞ける	*kikō* 聞こう	*kikareru* 聞かれる	*kikaseru* 聞かせる
kimattara 決まったら	— —	*kimarō* 決まろう	— —	— —
kittara 切ったら	*kireru* 切れる	*kirō* 切ろう	*kirareru* 切られる	*kiraseru* 切らせる
kondara 混んだら	— —	*komō* 混もう	— —	*komaseru* 混ませる
koroshitara 殺したら	*koroseru* 殺せる	*korosō* 殺そう	*korosareru* 殺される	*korosaseru* 殺させる
mattara 待ったら	*materu* 待てる	*matō* 待とう	*matareru* 待たれる	*mataseru* 待たせる
mottara 持ったら	*moteru* 持てる	*motō* 持とう	*motareru* 持たれる	*motaseru* 持たせる
naitara 泣いたら	*nakeru* 泣ける	*nakō* 泣こう	*nakareru* 泣かれる	*nakaseru* 泣かせる
naottara 直ったら	*naoreru* 直れる	*naorō* 直ろう	*naorareru* 直られる	*naoraseru* 直らせる
naoshitara 直したら	*naoseru* 直せる	*naosō* 直そう	*naosareru* 直される	*naosaseru* 直させる
narattara 習ったら	*naraeru* 習える	*naraō* 習おう	*narawareru* 習われる	*narawaseru* 習わせる
nattara なったら	*nareru* なれる	*narō* なろう	*narareru* なられる	*naraseru* ならせる

plain form	-*masu* form	-*te* form	-*nai* form	-*ta* form	-*ba* form
nokoru 残る remain (i)	*nokorimasu* 残ります	*nokotte* 残って	*nokoranai* 残らない	*nokotta* 残った	*nokoreba* 残れば
nomu 飲む drink	*nomimasu* 飲みます	*nonde* 飲んで	*nomanai* 飲まない	*nonda* 飲んだ	*nomeba* 飲めば
noru 乗る get on	*norimasu* 乗ります	*notte* 乗って	*noranai* 乗らない	*notta* 乗った	*noreba* 乗れば
nusumu 盗む steal	*nusumimasu* 盗みます	*nusunde* 盗んで	*nusumanai* 盗まない	*nusunda* 盗んだ	*nusumeba* 盗めば
okosu 起こす wake up (t)	*okoshimasu* 起こします	*okoshite* 起こして	*okosanai* 起こさない	*okoshita* 起こした	*okoseba* 起こせば
oku 置く put on	*okimasu* 置きます	*oite* 置いて	*okanai* 置かない	*oita* 置いた	*okeba* 置けば
okuru 送る send	*okurimasu* 送ります	*okutte* 送って	*okuranai* 送らない	*okutta* 送った	*okureba* 送れば
omou 思う think	*omoimasu* 思います	*omotte* 思って	*omowanai* 思わない	*omotta* 思った	*omoeba* 思えば
otosu 落とす drop (t)	*otoshimasu* 落とします	*otoshite* 落として	*otosanai* 落とさない	*otoshita* 落とした	*otoseba* 落とせば
owaru 終わる finish (i)	*owarimasu* 終わります	*owatte* 終わって	*owaranai* 終わらない	*owatta* 終わった	*owareba* 終われば
oyogu 泳ぐ swim	*oyogimasu* 泳ぎます	*oyoide* 泳いで	*oyoganai* 泳がない	*oyoida* 泳いだ	*oyogeba* 泳げば
sagaru 下がる go down, step back, retire	*sagarimasu* 下がります	*sagatte* 下がって	*sagaranai* 下がらない	*sagatta* 下がった	*sagareba* 下がれば
saku 咲く bloom	*sakimasu* 咲きます	*saite* 咲いて	*sakanai* 咲かない	*saita* 咲いた	*sakeba* 咲けば

conditional	potential	volitional	passive	causative
nokottara 残ったら	*nokoreru* 残れる	*nokorō* 残ろう	*nokorareru* 残られる	*nokoraseru* 残らせる
nondara 飲んだら	*nomeru* 飲める	*nomō* 飲もう	*nomareru* 飲まれる	*nomaseru* 飲ませる
nottara 乗ったら	*noreru* 乗れる	*norō* 乗ろう	*norareru* 乗られる	*noraseru* 乗らせる
nusundara 盗んだら	*nusumeru* 盗める	*nusumō* 盗もう	*nusumareru* 盗まれる	*nusumaseru* 盗ませる
okoshitara 起こしたら	*okoseru* 起こせる	*okosō* 起こそう	*okosareru* 起こされる	*okosaseru* 起こさせる
oitara 置いたら	*okeru* 置ける	*okō* 置こう	*okareru* 置かれる	*okaseru* 置かせる
okuttara 送ったら	*okureru* 送れる	*okurō* 送ろう	*okurareru* 送られる	*okuraseru* 送らせる
omottara 思ったら	*omoeru* 思える	*omoō* 思おう	*omowareru* 思われる	*omowaseru* 思わせる
otoshitara 落としたら	*otoseru* 落とせる	*otosō* 落とそう	*otosareru* 落とされる	*otosaseru* 落とさせる
owattara 終わったら	*owareru* 終われる	*owarasō* 終わらそう	*owarareru* 終わられる	*owaraseru* 終わらせる
oyoidara 泳いだら	*oyogeru* 泳げる	*oyogō* 泳ごう	*oyogareru* 泳がれる	*oyogaseru* 泳がせる
sagattara 下がったら	*sagareru* 下がれる	*sagarō* 下がろう	*sagarareru* 下がられる	*sagaraseru* 下がらせる
saitara 咲いたら	*sakeru* 咲ける	*sakō* 咲こう	*sakareru* 咲かれる	*sakaseru* 咲かせる

plain form	-*masu* form	-*te* form	-*nai* form	-*ta* form	-*ba* form
shimaru 閉まる close (i)	*shimarimasu* 閉まります	*shimatte* 閉まって	*shimaranai* 閉まらない	*shimatta* 閉まった	*shimareba* 閉まれば
shiru 知る know	*shirimasu* 知ります	*shitte* 知って	*shiranai* 知らない	*shitta* 知った	*shireba* 知れば
sugosu 過ごす pass (t)	*sugoshimasu* 過ごします	*sugoshite* 過ごして	*sugosanai* 過ごさない	*sugoshita* 過ごした	*sugoseba* 過ごせば
susumu 進む advance, go ahead	*susumimasu* 進みます	*susunde* 進んで	*susumanai* 進まない	*susunda* 進んだ	*susumeba* 進めば
suwaru 座る sit down	*suwarimasu* 座ります	*suwatte* 座って	*suwaranai* 座らない	*suwatta* 座った	*suwareba* 座れば
tatsu 立つ stand up	*tachimasu* 立ちます	*tatte* 立って	*tatanai* 立たない	*tatta* 立った	*tateba* 立てば
tomaru 止まる stop (i)	*tomarimasu* 止まります	*tomatte* 止まって	*tomaranai* 止まらない	*tomatta* 止まった	*tomareba* 止まれば
toru 取る pick up, take	*torimasu* 取ります	*totte* 取って	*toranai* 取らない	*totta* 取った	*toreba* 取れば
tsukau 使う use	*tsukaimasu* 使います	*tsukatte* 使って	*tsukawanai* 使わない	*tsukatta* 使った	*tsukaeba* 使えば
tsukuru 作る make	*tsukurimasu* 作ります	*tsukutte* 作って	*tsukuranai* 作らない	*tsukutta* 作った	*tsukureba* 作れば
uru 売る sell	*urimasu* 売ります	*utte* 売って	*uranai* 売らない	*utta* 売った	*ureba* 売れば
utau 歌う sing	*utaimasu* 歌います	*utatte* 歌って	*utawanai* 歌わない	*utatta* 歌った	*utaeba* 歌えば
wakaru 分かる understand	*wakarimasu* 分かります	*wakatte* 分かって	*wakaranai* 分からない	*wakatta* 分かった	*wakareba* 分かれば

conditional	potential	volitional	passive	causative
shimattara 閉まったら	— —	*shimarō* 閉まろう	— —	— —
shittara 知ったら	*shireru* 知れる	*shirō* 知ろう	*shirareru* 知られる	*shiraseru* 知らせる
sugoshitara 過ごしたら	*sugoseru* 過ごせる	*sugosō* 過ごそう	*sugosareru* 過ごされる	*sugosaseru* 過ごさせる
susundara 進んだら	*susumeru* 進める	*susumō* 進もう	*susumareru* 進まれる	*susumaseru* 進ませる
suwattara 座ったら	*suwareru* 座われる	*suwarō* 座ろう	*suwarareru* 座られる	*suwaraseru* 座らせる
tattara 立ったら	*tateru* 立てる	*tatō* 立とう	*tatareru* 立たれる	*tataseru* 立たせる
tomattara 止まったら	*tomareru* 止まれる	*tomarō* 止まろう	*tomarareru* 止まられる	*tomaraseru* 止まらせる
tottara 取ったら	*toreru* 取れる	*torō* 取ろう	*torareru* 取られる	*toraseru* 取らせる
tsukattara 使ったら	*tsukaeru* 使える	*tsukaō* 使おう	*tsukawareru* 使われる	*tsukawaseru* 使わせる
tsukuttara 作ったら	*tsukureru* 作れる	*tsukurō* 作ろう	*tsukurareru* 作られる	*tsukuraseru* 作らせる
uttara 売ったら	*ureru* 売れる	*urō* 売ろう	*urareru* 売られる	*uraseru* 売らせる
utattara 歌ったら	*utaeru* 歌える	*utaō* 歌おう	*utawareru* 歌われる	*utawaseru* 歌わせる
wakattara 分ったら	— —	*wakarō* 分かろう	*wakarareru* 分かられる	*wakaraseru* 分からせる

plain form	-*masu* form	-*te* form	-*nai* form	-*ta* form	-*ba* form
yamu 止む stop (i)	*yamimasu* 止みます	*yande* 止んで	*yamanai* 止まない	*yanda* 止んだ	*yameba* 止めば
yaru やる do, give	*yarimasu* やります	*yatte* やって	*yaranai* やらない	*yatta* やった	*yareba* やれば
yasumu 休む rest	*yasumimasu* 休みます	*yasunde* 休んで	*yasumanai* 休まない	*yasunda* 休んだ	*yasumeba* 休めば
yomu 読む read	*yomimasu* 読みます	*yonde* 読んで	*yomanai* 読まない	*yonda* 読んだ	*yomeba* 読めば

Group 2

plain form	-*masu* form	-*te* form	-*nai* form	-*ta* form	-*ba* form
ageru 上げる give	*agemasu* 上げます	*agete* 上げて	*agenai* 上げない	*ageta* 上げた	*agereba* 上げれば
akeru 開ける open (t)	*akemasu* 開けます	*akete* 開けて	*akenai* 開けない	*aketa* 開けた	*akereba* 開ければ
arawareru 現れる appear (i) (表れる be expressed)	*arawaremasu* 現れます	*arawarete* 現れて	*arawarenai* 現れない	*arawareta* 現れた	*arawarereba* 現れれば
deru 出る go out (i)	*demasu* 出ます	*dete* 出て	*denai* 出ない	*deta* 出た	*dereba* 出れば
hajimeru 始める start, begin (t)	*hajimemasu* 始めます	*hajimete* 始めて	*hajimenai* 始めない	*hajimeta* 始めた	*hajimereba* 始めれば
ireru 入れる put in (t)	*iremasu* 入れます	*irete* 入れて	*irenai* 入れない	*ireta* 入れた	*irereba* 入れれば
iru いる exist	*imasu* います	*ite* いて	*inai* いない	*ita* いた	*ireba* いれば

conditional	potential	volitional	passive	causative
yandara 止んだら	— —	*yamō* 止もう	— —	*yamaseru* 止ませる
yattara やったら	*yareru* やれる	*yarō* やろう	*yarareru* やられる	*yaraseru* やらせる
yasundara 休んだら	*yasumeru* 休める	*yasumō* 休もう	*yasumareru* 休まれる	*yasumaseru* 休ませる
yondara 読んだら	*yomeru* 読める	*yomō* 読もう	*yomareru* 読まれる	*yomaseru* 読ませる

conditional	potential	volitional	passive	causative
agetara 上げたら	*agerareru* 上げられる	*ageyō* 上げよう	*agerareru* 上げられる	*agesaseru* 上げさせる
aketara 開けたら	*akerareru* 開けられる	*akeyō* 開けよう	*akerareru* 開けられる	*akesaseru* 開けさせる
arawaretara 現れたら	*arawarerareru* 現れられる	*arawareyō* 現れよう	*arawarerareru* 現れられる	*arawaresaseru* 現れさせる
detara 出たら	*derareru* 出られる	*deyō* 出よう	*derareru* 出られる	*desaseru* 出させる
hajimetara 始めたら	*hajimerareru* 始められる	*hajimeyō* 始めよう	*hajimerareru* 始められる	*hajimesaseru* 始めさせる
iretara 入れたら	*irerareru* 入れられる	*ireyō* 入れよう	*irerareru* 入れられる	*iresaseru* 入れさせる
itara いたら	*irareru* いられる	*iyō* いよう	*irareru* いられる	*isaseru* いさせる

plain form	-*masu* form	-*te* form	-*nai* form	-*ta* form	-*ba* form
kaeru 変える change	*kaemasu* 変えます	*kaete* 変えて	*kaenai* 変えない	*kaeta* 変えた	*kaereba* 変えれば
kakeru かける make a phone call, hang, spend time	*kakemasu* かけます	*kakete* かけて	*kakenai* かけない	*kaketa* かけた	*kakereba* かければ
kangaeru 考える think	*kangaemasu* 考えます	*kangaete* 考えて	*kangaenai* 考えない	*kangaeta* 考えた	*kangaereba* 考えれば
kikoeru 聞こえる can be heard	*kikoemasu* 聞こえます	*kikoete* 聞こえて	*kikoenai* 聞こえない	*kikoeta* 聞こえた	*kikoereba* 聞こえれば
kimeru 決める decide	*kimemasu* 決めます	*kimete* 決めて	*kimenai* 決めない	*kimeta* 決めた	*kimereba* 決めれば
kiru 着る put on	*kimasu* 着ます	*kite* 着て	*kinai* 着ない	*kita* 着た	*kireba* 着れば
kureru くれる be given	*kuremasu* くれます	*kurete* くれて	*kurenai* くれない	*kureta* くれた	*kurereba* くれれば
miru 見る see, look	*mimasu* 見ます	*mite* 見て	*minai* 見ない	*mita* 見た	*mireba* 見れば
neru 寝る sleep	*nemasu* 寝ます	*nete* 寝て	*nenai* 寝ない	*neta* 寝た	*nereba* 寝れば
niru 似る resemble, look like	*nimasu* 似ます	*nite* 似て	*ninai* 似ない	*nita* 似た	*nireba* 似れば
noseru 乗せる put something on, place on the top of (t)	*nosemasu* 乗せます	*nosete* 乗せて	*nosenai* 乗せない	*noseta* 乗せた	*nosereba* 乗せれば
ochiru 落ちる fall, drop (i)	*ochimasu* 落ちます	*ochite* 落ちて	*ochinai* 落ちない	*ochita* 落ちた	*ochireba* 落ちれば
oeru 終える finish, end (t)	*oemasu* 終えます	*oete* 終えて	*oenai* 終えない	*oeta* 終えた	*oereba* 終えれば

conditional	potential	volitional	passive	causative
kaetara 変えたら	*kaerareru* 変えられる	*kaeyō* 変えよう	*kaerareru* 変えられる	*kaesaseru* 変えさせる
kaketara かけたら	*kakerareru* かけられる	*kakeyō* かけよう	*kakerareru* かけられる	*kakesaseru* かけさせる
kangaetara 考えたら	*kangaerareru* 考えられる	*kangaeyō* 考えよう	*kangaerareru* 考えられる	*kangaesaseru* 考えさせる
kikoetara 聞こえたら	— —	*kikoeyō* 聞こえよう	— —	— —
kimetara 決めたら	*kimerareru* 決められる	*kimeyō* 決めよう	*kimerareru* 決められる	*kimesaseru* 決めさせる
kitara 着たら	*kirareru* 着られる	*kiyō* 着よう	*kirareru* 着られる	*kisaseru* 着させる
kuretara くれたら	*kurerareru* くれられる	*kureyō* くれよう	*kurerareru* くれられる	*kuresaseru* くれさせる
mitara 見たら	*mirareru* 見られる	*miyō* 見よう	*mirareru* 見られる	*miraseru* 見らせる
netara 寝たら	*nerareru* 寝られる	*neyō* 寝よう	*nerareru* 寝られる	*nesaseru* 寝させる
nitara 似たら	*nirareru* 似られる	*niyō* 似よう	*nirareru* 似られる	*nisaseru* 似させる
nosetara 乗せたら	*noserareru* 乗せられる	*noseyō* 乗せよう	*noserareru* 乗せられる	*nosesaseru* 乗せさせる
ochitara 落ちたら	*ochirareru* 落ちられる	*ochiyō* 落ちよう	*ochirareru* 落ちられる	*ochiraseru* 落ちらせる
oetara 終えたら	*oerareru* 終えられる	*oeyō* 終えよう	*oerareru* 終えられる	*oesaseru* 終えさせる

plain form	-*masu* form	-*te* form	-*nai* form	-*ta* form	-*ba* form
okiru 起きる get up (i)	*okimasu* 起きます	*okite* 起きて	*okinai* 起きない	*okita* 起きた	*okireba* 起きれば
oriru 降りる get off (i)	*orimasu* 降ります	*orite* 降りて	*orinai* 降りない	*orita* 降りた	*orireba* 降りれば
oshieru 教える teach	*oshiemasu* 教えます	*oshiete* 教えて	*oshienai* 教えない	*oshieta* 教えた	*oshiereba* 教えれば
shimeru 閉める close, shut (t)	*shimemasu* 閉めます	*shimete* 閉めて	*shimenai* 閉めない	*shimeta* 閉めた	*shimereba* 閉めれば
shiraseru 知らせる tell, report	*shirasemasu* 知らせます	*shirasete* 知らせて	*shirasenai* 知らせない	*shiraseta* 知らせた	*shirasereba* 知らせれば
sugiru 過ぎる pass, be over (i)	*sugimasu* 過ぎます	*sugite* 過ぎて	*suginai* 過ぎない	*sugita* 過ぎた	*sugireba* 過ぎれば
suteru 捨てる throw away	*sutemasu* 捨てます	*sutete* 捨てて	*sutenai* 捨てない	*suteta* 捨てた	*sutereba* 捨てれば
taberu 食べる eat	*tabemasu* 食べます	*tabete* 食べて	*tabenai* 食べない	*tabeta* 食べた	*tabereba* 食べれば
tomeru 止める stop (t)	*tomemasu* 止めます	*tomete* 止めて	*tomenai* 止めない	*tometa* 止めた	*tomereba* 止めれば
tsukareru 疲れる get tired	*tsukaremasu* 疲れます	*tsukarete* 疲れて	*tsukarenai* 疲れない	*tsukareta* 疲れた	*tsukarereba* 疲れれば
tsutomeru 勤める work for	*tsutomemasu* 勤めます	*tsutomete* 勤めて	*tsutomenai* 勤めない	*tsutometa* 勤めた	*tsutomereba* 勤めれば
tsuzukeru 続ける continue (t)	*tsuzukemasu* 続けます	*tsuzukete* 続けて	*tsuzukenai* 続けない	*tsuzuketa* 続けた	*tsuzukereba* 続ければ
wasureru 忘れる forget	*wasuremasu* 忘れます	*wasurete* 忘れて	*wasurenai* 忘れない	*wasureta* 忘れた	*wasurereba* 忘れれば

conditional	potential	volitional	passive	causative
okitara 起きたら	okirareru 起きられる	okiyō 起きよう	okirareru 起きられる	okisaseru 起きさせる
oritara 降りたら	orirareru 降りられる	oriyō 降りよう	orirareru 降りられる	orisaseru 降りさせる
oshietara 教えたら	oshierareru 教えられる	oshieyō 教えよう	oshierareru 教えられる	oshiesaseru 教えさせる
shimetara 閉めたら	shimerareru 閉められる	shimeyō 閉めよう	shimerareru 閉められる	shimesaseru 閉めさせる
shirasetara 知らせたら	shiraserareru 知らせられる	shiraseyō 知らせよう	shiraserareru 知らせられる	shirasesaseru 知らせさせる
sugitara 過ぎたら	sugirareru 過ぎられる	sugiyō 過ぎよう	sugirareru 過ぎられる	sugiraseru 過ぎさせる
sutetara 捨てたら	suterareru 捨てられる	suteyō 捨てよう	suterareru 捨てられる	sutesaseru 捨てさせる
tabetara 食べたら	taberareru 食べられる	tabeyō 食べよう	taberareru 食べられる	tabesaseru 食べさせる
tometara 止めたら	tomerareru 止められる	tomeyō . 止めよう	tomerareru 止められる	tomesaseru 止めさせる
tsukaretara 疲れたら	tsukarerareru 疲れられる	tsukareyō 疲れよう	― ―	tsukaresaseru 疲れさせる
tsutometara 勤めたら	tsutomerareru 勤められる	tsutomeyō 勤めよう	tsutomerareru 勤められる	tsutomesaseru 勤めさせる
tsuzuketara 続けたら	tsuzukerareru 続けられる	tsuzukeyō 続けよう	tsuzukerareru 続けられる	tsuzukesaseru 続けさせる
wasuretara 忘れたら	wasurerareru 忘れられる	wasureyō 忘れよう	wasurerareru 忘れられる	wasuresaseru 忘れさせる

yameru	yamemasu	yamete	yamenai	yameta	yamereba
やめる	やめます	やめて	やめない	やめた	やめれば
quit, stop (t)					

Group 3 ———————————————————————

plain form	-*masu* form	-*te* form	-*nai* form	-*ta* form	-*ba* form
kuru	kimasu	kite	konai	kita	kureba
来る	来ます	来て	来ない	来た	来れば
come					
suru	shimasu	shite	shinai	shita	sureba
する	します	して	しない	した	すれば
do					

yametara やめたら	*yamerareru* やめられる	*yameyō* やめよう	*yamerareru* やめられる	*yamesaseru* やめさせる

conditional	potential	volitional	passive	causative
kitara 来たら	*korareru* 来られる	*koyō* 来よう	*korareru* 来られる	*kosaseru* 来させる
shitara したら	*dekiru* できる ②	*shiyō* しよう	*sareru* される	*saseru* させる

Adjective Inflection Chart—I-Adjectives

plain	stem	polite	-*te* form	negative
akai 赤い red	*aka* 赤	*akai desu* 赤いです	*aka-kute* 赤くて	*aka-ku nai* 赤くない
amai 甘い sweet	*ama* 甘	*amai desu* 甘いです	*ama-kute* 甘くて	*ama-ku nai* 甘くない
atsui 暑い hot	*atsu* 暑	*atsui desu* 暑いです	*atsu-kute* 暑くて	*atsu-ku nai* 暑くない
chiisai 小さい small / little	*chiisa* 小さ	*chiisai desu* 小さいです	*chiisa-kute* 小さくて	*chiisa-ku nai* 小さくない
chikai 近い near	*chika* 近	*chikai desu* 近いです	*chika-kute* 近くて	*chika-ku nai* 近くない
furui 古い old	*furu* 古	*furui desu* 古いです	*furu-kute* 古くて	*furu-ku nai* 古くない
hosoi 細い slim	*hoso* 細	*hosoi desu* 細いです	*hoso-kute* 細くて	*hoso-ku nai* 細くない
isogashii 忙しい busy	*isogashi* 忙し	*isogashii desu* 忙しいです	*isogashi-kute* 忙しくて	*isogashi-ku nai* 忙しくない
ii (irregular) いい good	*yo* よ	*ii desu* いいです	*yo-kute* よくて	*yo-ku nai* よくない
kanashii 悲しい sad	*kanashi* 悲し	*kanashii desu* 悲しいです	*kanashi-kute* 悲しくて	*kanashi-ku nai* 悲しくない
kawaii 可愛い cute	*kawai* 可愛	*kawaii desu* 可愛いです	*kawai-kute* 可愛くて	*kawai-ku nai* 可愛くない

past	past negative	conditional (*-tara* / *-kereba*)
aka-katta 赤かった	*aka-ku nakatta* 赤くなかった	*aka-kattara / aka-kereba* 赤かったら / 赤ければ
ama-katta 甘かった	*ama-ku nakatta* 甘くなかった	*ama-kattara / ama-kereba* 甘かったら / 甘ければ
atsu-katta 暑かった	*atsu-ku nakatta* 暑くなかった	*atsu-kattara / atsu-kereba* 暑かったら / 暑ければ
chiisa-katta 小さかった	*chiisa-ku nakatta* 小さくなかった	*chiisa-kattara / chiisa-kereba* 小さかったら / 小さければ
chika-katta 近かった	*chika-ku nakatta* 近くなかった	*chika-kattara / chika-kereba* 近かったら / 近ければ
furu-katta 古かった	*furu-ku nakatta* 古くなかった	*furu-kattara / furu-kereba* 古かったら / 古ければ
hoso-katta 細かった	*hoso-ku nakatta* 細くなかった	*hoso-kattara / hoso-kereba* 細かったら / 細ければ
isogashi-katta 忙しかった	*isogashi-ku nakatta* 忙しくなかった	*isogashi-kattara / isogashi-kereba* 忙しかったら / 忙しければ
yo-katta よかった	*yo-ku nakatta* よくなかった	*yo-kattara / yo-kereba* よかったら / よければ
kanashi-katta 悲しかった	*kanashi-ku nakatta* 悲しくなかった	*kanashi-kattara / kanashi-kereba* 悲しかったら / 悲しければ
kawai-katta 可愛かった	*kawai-ku nakatta* 可愛くなかった	*kawai-kattara / kawai-kereba* 可愛かったら / 可愛ければ

plain	stem	polite	-te form	negative
komakai 細かい small, fine	*komaka* 細か	*komakai desu* 細かいです	*komaka-kute* 細かくて	*komaka-ku nai* 細かくない
kowai 怖い fearful	*kowa* 怖	*kowai desu* 怖いです	*kowa-kute* 怖くて	*kowa-ku nai* 怖くない
kurai 暗い dark	*kura* 暗	*kurai desu* 暗いです	*kura-kute* 暗くて	*kura-ku nai* 暗くない
kurushii 苦しい painful / hard	*kurushi* 苦し	*kurushii desu* 苦しいです	*kurushi-kute* 苦しくて	*kurushi-ku nai* 苦しくない
nagai 長い long	*naga* 長	*nagai desu* 長いです	*naga-kute* 長くて	*naga-ku nai* 長くない
nurui ぬるい lukewarm	*nuru* ぬる	*nurui desu* ぬるいです	*nuru-kute* ぬるくて	*nuru-ku nai* ぬるくない
oishii おいしい delicious	*oishi* おいし	*oishii desu* おいしいです	*oishi-kute* おいしくて	*oishi-ku nai* おいしくない
ōkii 大きい big	*ōki* 大き	*ōkii desu* 大きいです	*ōki-kute* 大きくて	*ōki-ku nai* 大きくない
omoi 重い heavy	*omo* 重	*omoi desu* 重いです	*omo-kute* 重くて	*omo-ku nai* 重くない
omoshiroi 面白い interesting	*omoshiro* 面白	*omoshiroi desu* 面白いです	*omoshiro-kute* 面白くて	*omoshiro-ku nai* 面白くない
osoi 遅い late / slow	*oso* 遅	*osoi desu* 遅いです	*oso-kute* 遅くて	*oso-ku nai* 遅くない
sabishii 寂しい lonely / forlorn	*sabishi* 寂し	*sabishii desu* 寂しいです	*sabishi-kute* 寂しくて	*sabishi-ku nai* 寂しくない

past	past negative	conditional (-*tara* / -*kereba*)
komaka-katta 細かかった	komaka-ku nakatta 細かくなかった	komaka-kattara / komaka-kereba 細かかったら / 細かければ
kowa-katta 怖かった	kowa-ku nakatta 怖くなかった	kowa-kattara / kowa-kereba 怖かったら / 怖ければ
kura-katta 暗かった	kura-ku nakatta 暗くなかった	kura-kattara / kura-kereba 暗かったら / 暗ければ
kurushi-katta 苦しかった	kurushi-ku nakatta 苦しくなかった	kurushi-kattara / kurushi-kereba 苦しかったら / 苦しければ
naga-katta 長かった	naga-ku nakatta 長くなかった	naga-kattara / naga-kereba 長かったら / 長ければ
nuru-katta ぬるかった	nuru-ku nakatta ぬるくなかった	nuru-kattara / nuru-kereba ぬるかったら / ぬるければ
oishi-katta おいしかった	oishi-ku nakatta おいしくなかった	oishi-kattara / oishi-kereba おいしかったら / おいしければ
ōki-katta 大きかった	ōki-ku nakatta 大きくなかった	ōki-kattara / ōki-kereba 大きかったら / 大きければ
omo-katta 重かった	omo-ku nakatta 重くなかった	omo-kattara / omo-kereba 重かったら / 重ければ
omoshiro-katta 面白かった	omoshiro-ku nakatta 面白くなかった	omoshiro-kattara / omoshiro-kereba 面白かったら / 面白ければ
oso-katta 遅かった	oso-ku nakatta 遅くなかった	oso-kattara / oso-kereba 遅かったら / 遅ければ
sabishi-katta 寂しかった	sabishi-ku nakatta 寂しくなかった	sabishi-kattara / sabishi-kereba 寂しかったら / 寂しければ

plain	stem	polite	-te form	negative
samui 寒い cold	*samu* 寒	*samui desu* 寒いです	*samu-kute* 寒くて	*samu-ku nai* 寒くない
takai 高い expensive / high / tall	*taka* 高	*takai desu* 高いです	*taka-kute* 高くて	*taka-ku nai* 高くない
wakai 若い young	*waka* 若	*wakai desu* 若いです	*waka-kute* 若くて	*waka-ku nai* 若くない
yasui 安い cheap	*yasu* 安	*yasui desu* 安いです	*yasu-kute* 安くて	*yasu-ku nai* 安くない

Na-Adjectives

plain	stem	polite	-te form	negative
anzen da 安全だ safe	*anzen* 安全	*anzen desu* 安全です	*anzen de* 安全で	*anzen dewa nai* 安全ではない
benri da 便利 convenient / handy	*benri* 便利	*benri desu* 便利です	*benri de* 便利で	*benri dewa nai* 便利ではない
fuben da 不便だ inconvenient	*fuben* 不便	*fuben desu* 不便です	*fuben de* 不便で	*fuben dewa nai* 不便ではない
genki da 元気だ lively / healthy	*genki* 元気	*genki desu* 元気です	*genki de* 元気で	*genki dewa nai* 元気ではない
heta da 下手だ not good / unskillful	*heta* 下手	*heta desu* 下手です	*heta de* 下手で	*heta dewa nai* 下手ではない

past	past negative	conditional (*-tara* / *-kereba*)
samu-katta 寒かった	*samu-ku nakatta* 寒くなかった	*samu-kattara* / *samu-kereba* 寒かったら / 寒ければ
taka-katta 高かった	*taka-ku nakatta* 高くなかった	*taka-kattara* / *taka-kereba* 高かったら / 高ければ
waka-katta 若かった	*waka-ku nakatta* 若くなかった	*waka-kattara* / *waka-kereba* 若かったら / 若ければ
yasu-katta 安かった	*yasu-ku nakatta* 安くなかった	*yasu-kattara* / *yasu-kereba* 安かったら / 安ければ

past	past negative	conditional (*dattara* / *-kereba*)
anzen datta 安全だった	*anzen dewa nakatta* 安全ではなかった	*anzen dattara* / *anzen nara* 安全だったら / 安全なら
benri datta 便利だった	*benri dewa nakatta* 便利ではなかった	*benri dattara* / *benri nara* 便利だったら / 便利なら
fuben datta 不便だった	*fuben dewa nakatta* 不便でなかった	*fuben dattara* / *fuben nara* 不便だったら / 不便なら
genki datta 元気だった	*genki dewa nakatta* 元気でなかった	*genki dattara* / *genki nara* 元気だったら / 元気なら
heta datta 下手だった	*heta dewa nakatta* 下手でなかった	*heta dattara* / *heta nara* 下手だったら / 下手なら

Na-adjectives   297

plain	stem	polite	*-te* form	negative
jōbu da 丈夫だ healthy / strong	*jōbu* 丈夫	*jōbu desu* 丈夫です	*jōbu de* 丈夫で	*jōbu dewa nai* 丈夫ではない
jōzu da 上手だ good / skillful	*jōzu* 上手	*jōzu desu* 上手です	*jōzu de* 上手で	*jōzu dewa nai* 上手ではない
kirei da きれいだ beautiful	*kirei* きれい	*kirei desu* きれいです	*kirei de* きれいで	*kirei dewa nai* きれいではない
shiawase da 幸せだ happy	*shiawase* 幸せ	*shiawase desu* 幸せです	*shiawase de* 幸せで	*shiawase dewa nai* 幸せではない
shitsurei da 失礼だ rude / impolite	*shitsurei* 失礼	*shitsurei desu* 失礼です	*shitsurei de* 失礼で	*shitsurei dewa nai* 失礼ではない
shizuka da 静かだ quiet / calm	*shizuka* 静か	*shizuka desu* 静かです	*shizuka de* 静かで	*shizuka dewa nai* 静かではない
suteki da すてきだ wonderful	*suteki* すてき	*suteki desu* すてきです	*suteki de* すてきで	*suteki dewa nai* すてきではない
yūmei da 有名だ famous	*yūmei* 有名	*yūmei desu* 有名です	*yūmei de* 有名で	*yūmei dewa nai* 有名ではない
kiken da 危険だ dangerous	*kiken* 危険	*kiken desu* 危険です	*kiken de* 危険で	*kiken dewa nai* 危険ではない

past	past negative	conditional (*dattara / -kereba*)
jōbu datta 丈夫だった	*jōbu dewa nakatta* 丈夫でなかった	*jōbu dattara / jōbu nara* 丈夫だったら / 丈夫なら
jōzu datta 上手だった	*jōzu dewa nakatta* 上手でなかった	*jōzu dattara / jōzu nara* 上手だったら / 上手なら
kirei datta きれいだった	*kirei dewa nakatta* きれいではなかった	*kirei dattara / kirei nara* きれいだったら / きれいなら
shiawase datta 幸せだった	*shiawase dewa nakatta* 幸せでなかった	*shiawase dattara / shiawase nara* 幸せだったら / 幸せなら
shitsurei datta 失礼だった	*shitsurei dewa nakatta* 失礼でなかった	*shitsurei dattara / shitsurei nara* 失礼だったら / 失礼なら
shizuka datta 静かだった	*shizuka dewa nakatta* 静かではなかった	*shizuka dattara / shizuka nara* 静かだったら / 静かなら
suteki datta すてきだった	*suteki dewa nakatta* すてきではなかった	*suteki dattara / suteki nara* すてきだったら / すてきなら
yūmei dattara 有名だったら	*yūmei dewa nakatta* 有名でなかった	*yūmei dattara / yūmei nara* 有名だったら / 有名なら
kiken datta 危険だった	*kiken dewa nakatta* 危険ではなかった	*kiken dattara / kiken nara* 危険だったら / 危険なら

INDEX

The principal purpose of this index is to provide the student with ways of locating basic patterns in addition to the extensive Table of Contents. Once the student has become familiar with the formulas used in this dictionary, the most efficient look-up method is by use of those formulas (for example, if you wish to check the pattern for the sentence *Kore wa hon desu*, you would look up *N1 wa N2 desu*). Since most of the patterns begin with the subject of the sentence (a noun), that means that most formulas begin with the letter N. However, since the subject is often dropped in Japanese, the index also list patterns with the subject dropped (for example, the pattern *N1 wa N2 ni N3 de N4 o V-masu* is also indexed as *N1 ni N2 de N3 o V-masu*, with an alteration in the superior numbers to reflect the changed order of words).

にほんご きほんぶんけいじてん
日本語基本文型辞典
A Dictionary of Basic Japanese Sentence Patterns

2000年4月　第1刷発行
2004年5月　第6刷発行

著　者　　茅野直子
　　　　　ち　の なお こ

発行者　　畑野文夫

発行所　　講談社インターナショナル株式会社
　　　　　〒112-8652　東京都文京区音羽 1-17-14
　　　　　電話　03-3944-6493（編集部）
　　　　　　　　03-3944-6492（営業部・業務部）
　　　　　ホームページ　www.kodansha-intl.co.jp

印刷・製本所　共同印刷株式会社

落丁本、乱丁本は購入書店名を明記のうえ、講談社インターナショナル業務部宛
にお送りください。送料小社負担にてお取替えいたします。なお、この本につい
てのお問い合わせは、編集部宛にお願いいたします。本書の無断複写（コピー）
は著作権法上での例外を除き、禁じられています。

定価はカバーに表示してあります。

The best-selling language course is now even better!

JAPANESE FOR BUSY PEOPLE Revised Edition

改訂版 コミュニケーションのための日本語 全3巻

Association for Japanese-Language Teaching (AJALT)

The leading textbook for conversational Japanese has been improved to make it easier than ever to teach and learn Japanese.

- Transition to advancing levels is more gradual.
- Kana version available for those who prefer Japanese script. Audio supplements compatible with both versions.
- English-Japanese glossary added to each volume.
- Short *kanji* lessons introduced in Volume II.
- Clearer explanations of grammar. • Shorter, easy-to-memorize dialogues.

Volume I

Teaches the basics for communication and provides a foundation for further study.

- Additional appendices for grammar usage.

Text	paperback, 232 pages	ISBN 4-7700-1882-7
Text / Kana Version	paperback, 256 pages	ISBN 4-7700-1987-4
Cassette Tapes	three cassette tapes (total 120 min.)	ISBN 4-7700-1883-5
Compact Discs	two compact discs (total 120 min.)	ISBN 4-7700-1909-2
The Workbook	paperback, 192 pages	ISBN 4-7700-1907-6
The Workbook Cassette Tapes	two cassette tapes (total 100 min.)	ISBN 4-7700-1769-3
Japanese Teacher's Manual	paperback, 160 pages	ISBN 4-7700-1906-8
English Teacher's Manual	paperback, 244 pages	ISBN 4-7700-1888-6

Volume II

Provides the basic language skills necessary to function in a professional environment.

Text	paperback, 288 pages	ISBN 4-7700-1884-3
Text / Kana Version	paperback, 296 pages	ISBN 4-7700-2051-1
Compact Discs	three compact discs (total 200 min.)	ISBN 4-7700-2136-4
The Workbook	paperback, 260 pages	ISBN 4-7700-2037-6
The Workbook Cassette Tapes	three cassette tapes (total 130 min.)	ISBN 4-7700-2111-9
Japanese Teacher's Manual	paperback, 168 pages	ISBN 4-7700-2036-8

Volume III

Expands vocabulary and structure to bring the student to the intermediate level.

Text	paperback, 256 pages	ISBN 4-7700-1886-X
Text / Kana Version	paperback, 296 pages	ISBN 4-7700-2052-X
Compact Discs	three compact discs (total 200 min.)	ISBN 4-7700-2137-2
The Workbook	paperback, 288 pages	ISBN 4-7700-2331-6
The Workbook Cassette Tapes	two cassette tapes (total 100 min.)	ISBN 4-7700-2358-8
Japanese Teacher's Manual	paperback, 200 pages	ISBN 4-7700-2306-5

Kana Workbook

Straightforward text for quick mastery of *hiragana* and *katakana* utilizing parallel learning of reading, writing, listening, and pronunciation.

- Grids for writing practice. • Reading and writing exercises.
- Optional audio tape aids in pronunciation.

Text	paperback, 80 pages	ISBN 4-7700-2096-1
Cassette Tape	one cassette tape (40 min.)	ISBN 4-7700-2097-X

INNOVATIVE WORKBOOKS FOR LEARNING JAPANESE KANA & KANJI

LET'S LEARN HIRAGANA　ひらがな
Yasuko Kosaka Mitamura

A well-tested, step-by-step program for individual study of the *hiragana* syllabary.

Paperback, 72 pages; ISBN 0-87011-709-2

LET'S LEARN KATAKANA　カタカナ
Yasuko Kosaka Mitamura

The companion volume for learning the *katakana* syllabary used for foreign words and new terms.

Paperback, 88 pages; ISBN 0-87011-719-X

LET'S LEARN KANJI　漢字を勉強しましょう
Yasuko Kosaka Mitamura and Joyce Mitamura

An innovative approach to learning the basic components of *kanji*, demonstrating simply how a finite number of parts combine into a wide variety of characters.

Paperback, 272 pages; ISBN 4-7700-2068-6

DECODING KANJI　A Practical Approach to Learning Look-Alike Characters
速習・漢字ブック
Yaeko S. Habein with the assistance of Gerald B. Mathias

Through judicious explanation and numerous exercises, this unique approach to learning similar *kanji* helps the student differentiate and, more importantly, remember these difficult characters. Several indices also make this a valuable reference tool.

Paperback, 144 pages; ISBN 4-7700-2498-3

KODANSHA INTERNATIONAL DICTIONARIES

Easy-to-use dictionaries designed for non-native learners of Japanese.

KODANSHA'S FURIGANA JAPANESE DICTIONARY
JAPANESE-ENGLISH / ENGLISH-JAPANESE　ふりがな和英・英和辞典

Both of Kodansha's popular furigana dictionaries in one portable, affordable volume. A truly comprehensive and practical dictionary for English-speaking learners, and an invaluable guide to using the Japanese language.
- 30,000-word basic vocabulary　• Hundreds of special words, names, and phrases
- Clear explanations of semantic and usage differences　• Special information on grammar and usage

Hardcover, 1318 pages; ISBN 4-7700-2480-0

KODANSHA'S FURIGANA JAPANESE-ENGLISH DICTIONARY

新装版 ふりがな和英辞典

The essential dictionary for all students of Japanese.
- Furigana readings added to all *kanji*　• 16,000-word basic vocabulary

Paperback, 592 pages; ISBN 4-7700-2750-8

KODANSHA'S FURIGANA ENGLISH-JAPANESE DICTIONARY

新装版 ふりがな英和辞典

The companion to the essential dictionary for all students of Japanese.
- Furigana readings added to all *kanji*　• 14,000-word basic vocabulary

Paperback, 728 pages; ISBN 4-7700-2751-6

KODANSHA'S ROMANIZED JAPANESE-ENGLISH DICTIONARY

新装版 ローマ字和英辞典

A portable reference written for beginning and intermediate students.
- 16,000-word basic vocabulary　• No knowledge of *kanji* necessary.

Paperback, 688 pages; ISBN 4-7700-2753-2

KODANSHA'S CONCISE ROMANIZED JAPANESE-ENGLISH DICTIONARY

コンサイス版 ローマ字和英辞典

A first, basic dictionary for beginner students of Japanese.
- 10,000-word basic vocabulary　• Easy-to-find romanized entries listed in alphabetical order
- Definitions written for English-speaking users
- Sample sentences in romanized and standard Japanese script, followed by English translations

Paperback, 480 pages; ISBN 4-7700-2849-0

KODANSHA'S BASIC ENGLISH-JAPANESE DICTIONARY

日本語学習 基礎英日辞典

An annotated dictionary useful for both students and teachers.
- Over 4,500 headwords and 18,000 vocabulary items　• Examples and information on stylistic differences
- Appendices for technical terms, syntax and grammar

Paperback , 1520 pages; ISBN 4-7700-2895-4

THE MODERN ENGLISH-NIHONGO DICTIONARY

日本語学習 英日辞典

The first truly bilingual dictionary designed exclusively for non-native learners of Japanese.
- Over 6,000 headwords　• Both standard Japanese (with *furigana*) and romanized orthography
- Sample sentences provided for most entries　• Numerous explanatory notes and *kanji* guides

Vinyl flexibinding, 1200 pages; ISBN 4-7700-2148-8

KODANSHA INTERNATIONAL DICTIONARIES
Easy-to-use dictionaries designed for non-native learners of Japanese.

KODANSHA'S ELEMENTARY KANJI DICTIONARY
新装版 教育漢英熟語辞典

A first, basic *kanji* dictionary for non-native learners of Japanese.
• Complete guide to 1,006 *Shin-kyōiku kanji*   • Over 10,000 common compounds
• Three indices for finding *kanji*   • Compact, portable format   • Functional, up-to-date, timely
Paperback, 576 pages; ISBN 4-7700-2752-4

KODANSHA'S ESSENTIAL KANJI DICTIONARY
新装版 常用漢英熟語辞典

A functional character dictionary that is both compact and comprehensive.
• Complete guide to the 1,945 essential *jōyō kanji*   • 20,000 common compounds
• Three indices for finding *kanji*
Paperback, 928 pages; ISBN 4-7700-2891-1

THE KODANSHA KANJI LEARNER'S DICTIONARY
新装版 漢英学習字典

The perfect kanji tool for beginners to advanced learners.
• Revolutionary SKIP lookup method   • Five lookup methods and three indices
• 2,230 entries & 41,000 meanings for 31,000 words
Paperback, 1060 pages (2-color); ISBN 4-7700-2855-5

KODANSHA'S EFFECTIVE JAPANESE USAGE DICTIONARY
新装版 日本語使い分け辞典

A concise, bilingual dictionary which clarifies the usage of frequently confused words and phrases.
• Explanations of 708 synonymous terms   • Numerous example sentences
Paperback, 768 pages; ISBN 4-7700-2850-4

KODANSHA'S DICTIONARY OF BASIC JAPANESE IDIOMS
日本語イディオム辞典

All idioms are given in Japanese script and romanized text with English translations. There are approximately 880 entries, many of which have several senses.
Paperback, 672 pages; ISBN 4-7700-2797-4

A DICTIONARY OF JAPANESE PARTICLES
てにをは辞典

Treats over 100 particles in alphabetical order, providing sample sentences for each meaning.
• Meets students' needs from beginning to advanced levels
• Treats principal particle meanings as well as variants
Paperback, 368 pages; ISBN 4-7700-2352-9

A DICTIONARY OF BASIC JAPANESE SENTENCE PATTERNS
日本語基本文型辞典

Author of the best-selling All About Particles explains fifty of the most common, basic patterns and their variations, along with numerous contextual examples. Both a reference and a textbook for students at all levels.
• Formulas delineating basic pattern structure   • Commentary on individual usages
Paperback, 320 pages; ISBN 4-7700-2608-0

www.thejapanpage.com

JAPANESE LANGUAGE GUIDES

Easy-to-use guides to essential language skills

13 SECRETS FOR SPEAKING FLUENT JAPANESE

日本語をペラペラ話すための13の秘訣　*Giles Murray*

The most fun, rewarding, and universal techniques of successful learners of Japanese that anyone can put immediately to use. A unique and exciting alternative, full of lively commentaries, comical illustrations, and brain-teasing puzzles.

Paperback, 184 pages; ISBN 4-7700-2302-2

ALL ABOUT PARTICLES　　新装版 助詞で変わるあなたの日本語　*Naoko Chino*

The most common and less common particles brought together and broken down into some 200 usages, with abundant sample sentences.

Paperback, 160 pages; ISBN 4-7700-2781-8

JAPANESE VERBS AT A GLANCE　　新装版 日本語の動詞　*Naoko Chino*

Clear and straightforward explanations of Japanese verbs—their functions, forms, roles, and politeness levels.

Paperback, 180 pages; ISBN 4-7700-2765-6

BEYOND POLITE JAPANESE: A Dictionary of Japanese Slang and Colloquialisms

新装版 役に立つ話しことば辞典　*Akihiko Yonekawa*

Expressions that all Japanese, but few foreigners, know and use every day. Sample sentences for every entry.

Paperback, 176 pages; ISBN 4-7700-2773-7

BUILDING WORD POWER IN JAPANESE: Using Kanji Prefixes and Suffixes

新装版 増えて使えるヴォキャブラリー　*Timothy J. Vance*

Expand vocabulary and improve reading comprehension by modifying your existing lexicon.

Paperback, 128 pages; ISBN 4-7700-2799-0

HOW TO SOUND INTELLIGENT IN JAPANESE: A Vocabulary Builder

新装版 日本語の知的表現　*Charles De Wolf*

Lists, defines, and gives examples for the vocabulary necessary to engage in intelligent conversation in fields such as politics, art, literature, business, and science.

Paperback, 160 pages; ISBN 4-7700-2859-8

MAKING SENSE OF JAPANESE: What the Textbooks Don't Tell You

新装版 日本語の秘訣　*Jay Rubin*

"Brief, wittily written essays that gamely attempt to explain some of the more frustrating hurdles [of Japanese].… They can be read and enjoyed by students at any level."　　—*Asahi Evening News*

Paperback, 144 pages; ISBN 4-7700-2802-4

LOVE, HATE and Everything in Between: Expressing Emotions in Japanese

新装版 日本語の感情表現集　*Mamiko Murakami*

Includes more than 400 phrases that are useful when talking about personal experience and nuances of feeling.

Paperback, 176 pages; ISBN 4-7700-2803-2

JAPANESE LANGUAGE GUIDES

Easy-to-use guides to essential language skills

THE HANDBOOK OF JAPANESE VERBS

日本語動詞ハンドブック　*Taeko Kamiya*

An indispensable reference and guide to Japanese verbs aimed at beginning and intermediate students. Precisely the book that verb-challenged students have been looking for.

• Verbs are grouped, conjugated, and combined with auxiliaries　• Different forms are used in sentences
• Each form is followed by reinforcing examples and exercises

Paperback, 256 pages; ISBN 4-7700-2683-8

THE HANDBOOK OF JAPANESE ADJECTIVES AND ADVERBS

日本語形容詞・副詞ハンドブック　*Taeko Kamiya*

The ultimate reference manual for those seeking a deeper understanding of Japanese adjectives and adverbs and how they are used in sentences. Ideal, too, for those simply wishing to expand their vocabulary or speak livelier Japanese.

Paperback , 336 pages; ISBN 4-7700-2879-2

A HANDBOOK OF COMMON JAPANESE PHRASES

日本語決まり文句辞典　*Sanseido*

Japanese is rich in common phrases perfect for any number and variety of occasions. This handbook lists some 600 of them and explains when, where, and how to use them, providing alternatives for slightly varied circumstances and revealing their underlying psychology.

Paperback, 320 pages; ISBN 4-7700-2798-2

BASIC CONNECTIONS: Making Your Japanese Flow

新装版 日本語の基礎ルール　*Kakuko Shoji*

Explains how words and phrases dovetail, how clauses pair up with other clauses, how sentences come together to create harmonious paragraphs. The goal is to enable the student to speak both coherently and smoothly.

Paperback, 160 pages; ISBN 4-7700-2860-1

JAPANESE CORE WORDS AND PHRASES: Things You Can't Find in a Dictionary

新装版 辞書では解らない慣用表現　*Kakuko Shoji*

Some Japanese words and phrases, even though they lie at the core of the language, forever elude the student's grasp. This book brings these recalcitrants to bay.

Paperback, 144 pages; ISBN 4-7700-2774-5

READ REAL JAPANESE: All You Need to Enjoy Eight Contemporary Writers

新装版 日本語で読もう　*Janet Ashby*

Original Japanese essays by Yoko Mori, Ryuichi Sakamoto, Machi Tawara, Shoichi Nejime, Momoko Sakura, Seiko Ito, Banana Yoshimoto, and Haruki Murakami. With vocabulary lists giving the English for Japanese words and phrases and also notes on grammar, nuance, and idiomatic usage.

Paperback, 168 pages; ISBN 4-7700-2936-5

BREAKING INTO JAPANESE LITERATURE: Seven Modern Classics in Parallel Text

日本語を読むための七つの物語　*Giles Murray*

Read classics of modern Japanese fiction in the original with the aid of a built-in, customized dictionary, free MP3 sound files of professional Japanese narrators reading the stories, and literal English translations. Features Ryunosuke Akutagawa's "Rashomon" and other stories.

Paperback, 240 pages; ISBN 4-7700-2899-7

JAPANESE LITERATURE

ANTHOLOGIES

HAIKU